The Double Flame

OCTAVIO PAZ

The Double Flame

LOVE AND EROTICISM

Translated from the Spanish by Helen Lane

HARCOURT BRACE & COMPANY

New York   San Diego   London

This is a translation of LA LLAMA DOBLE, AMOR Y EROTISMO

Library of Congress Cataloging-in-Publication Data
Paz, Octavio, 1914–
[Llama doble. English]
The double flame:love and eroticism/Octavio Paz: translated
from the Spanish by Helen Lane.
p.   cm.
ISBN 0-15-100103-0
1. Sex in literature.   2. Love in literature.   3. Erotic
literature—History and criticism.   I. Title.
PN56.S5P3913   1995
809'.933538—dc20   94-32282

Designed by Lori J. McThomas
Printed in the United States of America
First U.S. edition
A B C D E

CONTENTS

Preface

WHEN DOES A book begin to be written? How much
time does it take to write? Seemingly easy questions; in
reality, difficult ones. Going by the external facts, I began this book in early March and finished it at the end
of April: two months. The truth is that it was begun
in my adolescence. My first poems were love poems,
and love has appeared in my poetry ever since. I was
also an avid reader of tragedies and comedies, novels
and love poems, tales from *A Thousand and One Nights,
Romeo and Juliet, The Charterhouse of Parma.* This
reading nurtured my thoughts and illuminated my

experiences. In 1960 I wrote half a hundred pages on Sade, in which I tried to trace the boundaries between animal sexuality, human eroticism, and the more restricted domain of love. I was not entirely satisfied, but that essay served to make me realize the vastness of the subject. Around 1965, while I was living in India—the nights were as blue and electric as those of the poem that sings of the loves of Krishna and Radha—I fell in love. I decided to write a little book on love. Taking as its point of departure the intimate connections between the three domains—sex, eroticism, and love—it would be an exploration of the amatory feeling. I made a few notes, but had to stop: pressing tasks claimed my attention and forced me to postpone the project. I left India. Some ten years later, in the United States, I wrote an essay on Fourier in which I returned to some of the ideas outlined in my notes. Once again, other preoccupations and tasks intervened. My project became an increasingly remote possibility. I could not forget it, but neither did I feel able to carry it out.

Years went by. I continued to write poems. Often they were love poems, and in them there appeared, like recurrent musical phrases—like obsessions, even—images that were the crystallization of my thoughts. It will not be difficult for a reader who has read some of my poems to find bridges and correspondences between them and these pages. To me, poetry and thought are a system of communicating vessels. The source of both is my life. I write about what I have lived and am living. To live is also to think, and sometimes to cross that border beyond which feeling and thinking become one: poetry. Meanwhile, the pages on which I had scrawled my notes in India turned yellow, and a number of them were lost in moves to new quarters and in my travels. I abandoned the idea of writing the book.

Last December, gathering together certain texts for a collection of essays (entitled *Ideas y costumbres,* Ideas and Customs), I remembered that abandoned book. I felt more than regret, I felt shame: this was not forgetfulness but a betrayal. I spent several sleepless nights gnawed by remorse. I felt the need to return to my idea and complete it. But I held back: Wasn't it a little ridiculous, at the end of my days, to write a book about love? Or was this to be a farewell, a last testament? I shook my head, thinking that Quevedo, in my place, would have taken advantage of the occasion to write a satirical sonnet. I tried to think of other things, but it was useless: the book would not leave me in peace. Several weeks filled with doubts went by. Then suddenly one morning, I began to write with a sort of joyous desperation. I had planned on an essay of about a hundred pages, but as I wrote, new vistas appeared, and with urgent spontaneity the manuscript kept growing, until, with the same naturalness and the same urgency, the words stopped. I rubbed my eyes: I had written a book. My promise had been kept.

This book is intimately related to a poem I wrote a few years ago: "Carta de creencia." The title signifies the letter we carry with us so we may be believed by strangers: in this case, the majority of my readers. It can also mean a document containing the declaration of our beliefs, This, at least, is the meaning I attribute to it. Repeating a title, however, is aesthetically displeasing, and it gives rise to confusion. I therefore chose another title: *The Double Flame.* According to the *Diccionario de Autoridades,* the flame is "the most subtle part of fire, moving upward and raising itself above in the shape of a pyramid." The original, primordial fire, sexuality, raises the red flame of eroticism, and this in turn raises and feeds another flame, tremulous and blue: the flame of love. Eroticism and love: the double flame of life.

MEXICO CITY
May 4, 1993

The Kingdoms of Pan

PERCEPTIBLE REALITY HAS always been a source
of surprises to me. Of proofs as well. In a long-ago
article, written in 1940, I referred to poetry as "the testimony of the senses." True testimony: its images are
palpable, visible, and audible. To be sure, poetry is
made up of words linked together, which give off reflections, glints, iridescences. But what it shows us, are
they realities or illusions? Rimbaud said: "Et j'ai
quelquefois vu / ce que l'homme a cru voir" (And I
sometimes saw / what man believed he saw). Fusion of
seeing and *believing*. In the joining of these two words

lies the secret of poetry and its testimony: what the poem shows us we do not see with our carnal eyes but with the eyes of the spirit. Poetry lets us touch the impalpable and hear the tide of silence that covers a landscape devastated by insomnia. Poetic testimony reveals to us another world inside this world, the other world that is this world. The senses, without losing their powers, become servants of the imagination and let us hear the inaudible and see the invisible. But isn't this what happens in dreams and in the erotic encounter? When we dream and when we couple, we embrace phantoms. Each of the two who constitute the couple possesses a body, a face, and a name, but their real reality, precisely at the most intense moment of the embrace, disperses in a cascade of sensation which disperses in turn. There is a question that all lovers ask each other, and in it the erotic mystery is epitomized: Who are you? A question without an answer . . . The senses are and are not of this world. By means of them, poetry traces a bridge between *seeing* and *believing*. By that bridge, imagination is embodied and bodies turn into images.

The relationship between eroticism and poetry is such that it can be said, without affectation, that the former is a poetry of the body and the latter an eroticism of language. They are in complementary opposition. Language—sound that carries meanings, a material trace that denotes nonmaterial things—is able to give a name to what is most fleeting and evanescent: sensation. Nor is eroticism mere animal sexuality; it is ceremony, representation. It is sexuality transfigured, a metaphor. The agent that provokes both the erotic act and the poetic act is imagination. Imagination turns sex into ceremony and rite, language into rhythm and metaphor. The poetic image is an embrace of opposite realities, and rhyme a copulation of sounds; poetry eroticizes language and the world, because its operation is erotic to begin with. Likewise eroticism is a metaphor of animal sexuality. What does this metaphor say? Like all metaphors, it points to something that is beyond the reality that gave rise to it, something new and different from the terms that it comprises. If Góngora says "blood-red snowfall," he invents or discovers a reality that, though containing both, is neither blood nor snow. The same happens with eroticism: it says, or, rather, *it is*, something different from mere sexuality.

Although there are any number of ways of copulating, the sex act always says the same thing: reproduction. Eroticism is sex in action, but, because it either diverts it or denies it, it thwarts the goal of the sexual function. In sexuality, pleasure serves procreation; in erotic rituals, pleasure is an end in itself or has ends other than procreation. Sterility is not only a frequent note in eroticism but in certain ceremonies it is one of its conditions. Gnostic and Tantric texts repeatedly speak of semen being retained by the officiating priest or being poured out on the altar. In sexuality, violence and aggression are necessary components of copulation and therefore of reproduction; in eroticism, aggression ceases to serve reproduction and becomes an end in itself. In short, while the sexual metaphor through all its variations always says reproduction, the erotic metaphor, indifferent to the perpetuation of life, places reproduction between brackets.

The relationship of poetry to language resembles that of eroticism to sexuality. In like manner, in the poem —a verbal crystallization—language deviates from its natural end, communication. Language is naturally linear; words follow one after the other like running water. In a poem, linearity twists back on itself, retraces its steps, meanders; the straight line ceases to be the archetype and is replaced by the circle and the spiral. There is a moment when language ceases to crawl and rises to its feet and teeters above empty space; and there is a moment when it ceases to move and transforms itself into a transparent solid—a cube, sphere, obelisk

—firmly planted in the center of the page. Meanings converge or diverge; either way, they cancel themselves out. Words do not say the same things they do in prose; the poem no longer aspires to say, only to be. Poetry places communication in brackets in the same way that eroticism brackets reproduction.

Confronted with hermetic poems, we ask ourselves in bewilderment: What are they saying? If we read a simple poem, our perplexity disappears, but not our amazement: Is this limpid language—water, air—the same one in which books on sociology and newspapers are written? Later, when we have overcome our amazement, though not our enchantment, we discover that the poem presents us with another sort of communication, one governed by laws different from those that rule the exchange of news and information. The language of the poem is everyday language, yet that everyday language says things quite out of the ordinary. This is the reason for the mistrust all churches have for the poetry of mystics. St. John of the Cross did not wish to say anything that departed from the teachings of the Church; nonetheless, his poems said other things. Any number of examples of this could be given. The dangerous nature of poetry is inherent in its composition and is a constant in all periods and in all poets. There is always a schism between social and poetic expression: poetry is the *other* voice, as I have put it in another text. Therefore its correspondence with the aspects—both black and white—to which I have referred is at once natural and disturbing. Poetry and eroticism originate in the senses but do not end in them. As they unfold, they invent imaginary configurations: poems and ceremonies.

I DO NOT propose to dwell on the affinities between poetry and eroticism. I have explored that subject on other occasions; I raise it here only to introduce a different subject, though one intimately associated with poetry: love. First, it is necessary to distinguish love, properly speaking, from both eroticism and sexuality. The relationships between these are so close that they are frequently confused. For example, we sometimes speak of the love life of such and such a man or woman, but what we really mean is their erotic life. When Swann and Odette spoke of *faire cattleya*, they were referring not only to copulation. As Proust points out: "That particular way of saying *to make love* did not mean to them precisely the same thing as its synonyms." The erotic act becomes detached from the sex act: it is sex and it is something else besides. Moreover, the

talisman-word *cattleya* had one meaning for Odette and
another for Swann: to her it was a certain erotic pleasure with a certain person, and to him it was a harrow-
ing and painful sentiment—the love he felt for Odette.
The confusion is not to be wondered at: sex, eroticism,
and love are aspects of the same phenomenon, manifestations of what we call life. The oldest of the three,
the most comprehensive and most basic, is sex. Sex is
the primordial source. Eroticism and love are forms de-
rived from the sexual instinct: crystallizations, sublima-
tions, perversions, and condensations which transform
sexuality, very often into something unknowable. As in
the case of concentric circles, sex is the center and pivot
point of this geometry of passion.

The domain of sex, though the vastest of the three,
is but a small province in an even larger kingdom—
that of animate matter. Which in turn is but a minus-
cule part of the universe. It is quite likely, though we
do not know for certain, that in other solar systems of
other galaxies there are planets that have life forms
similar to ours; yet however numerous such planets
may be, life will remain an infinitesimal part of the
universe, an exception. As modern science conceives of
it, the universe is a totality of galaxies in continual expansion. But the laws that govern that expansion are

apparently not wholly applicable to the world of elementary particles. And within this division, another makes its appearance: animate matter. The second law of thermodynamics, the tendency toward entropy, yields to a reverse process: evolution, differentiated organisms, and the constant production of new species. The arrow of biology is loosed in a direction opposite to that of the arrow of physics. At this juncture yet another exception arises: cells multiply by splitting, by budding, or by parthenogenesis, but there is a small island of life in which reproduction takes place through the union of germ cells, gametes. This is the island of sexuality, and its domain is a limited one, encompassing the animal kingdom and some species of the vegetable kingdom. Humankind shares with animals and certain plants the need to reproduce sexually and not by the simpler method of self-division.

Once the borders of sexuality have been roughly sketched, we can draw the line that divides it from eroticism—a sinuous line and one fairly often trespassed, either by a violent surge of the sexual instinct or by incursions of erotic fantasy. Eroticism is, above all else, exclusively human: it is sexuality socialized and transfigured by the imagination and the will of human beings. The first thing that distinguishes eroticism from sexuality is the infinite variety of forms in which it manifests itself. Eroticism is invention, constant variation; sex is always the same. The protagonist of the erotic act is sex, or, to be more precise, the sexes. The plural is essential, because even in the so-called solitary pleasures sexual desire always invents an imaginary other . . . or many others. Also, in every erotic encounter there is an invisible and ever-active participant: imagination, desire. In the erotic act it is always two or more—never just one—who take part. Here the first difference between animal sexuality and human eroticism makes its appearance: in the latter, one or several of the players can be an imaginary being. Only humans copulate with incubi and succubi.

The basic positions, according to the ancients and Julio Romano's engravings, are twelve in number, but erotic ceremonies and games are innumerable and continually change through the action of desire, the father of fantasy. Eroticism varies in accordance with climate and geography, with societies and history, with individuals and temperaments. And with opportunity, chance, and the inspiration of the moment. If humans are "undulating" creatures, the sea in which they are rocked to and fro is set in motion by the capricious waves of eroticism. This is another difference between sexuality and eroticism. Animals always copulate in the same way; humans look at themselves in the mirror of universal animal copulation, and as they imitate it, they transform it and their own sexuality. However odd animal copulations may be, some tender and some fierce, there is no variation in them. The male dove coos and circles the female; the female praying mantis devours the male once she is fertilized. A terrifying and prodigious monotony, which in the human world becomes a terrifying and prodigious diversity.

In the heart of nature, humans have created for themselves a world apart, composed of this entirety of practices, institutions, rites, ideas, and artifacts that we call culture. By origin, eroticism is sex, nature; by its being a human creation and by its functions in society, it is culture. One of the aims of eroticism is to take sex and make a place for it in society. Without sex there can be no society, since there can be no procreation; but sex also threatens society. Like the god Pan, it is creation and destruction. It is instinct: tremors, panic, the explosion of life. It is a volcano and any one of its eruptions can bury society under a violent flow of blood and semen. Sex is subversive: it ignores classes and hierarchies, arts and sciences, day and night—it sleeps and awakens, only to fornicate and go back to sleep again.

Another difference from the animal world: our species suffers from an insatiable sexual thirst and does not experience, as do other animals, periods of rut and sexual dormancy. The human being is the only living creature that does not possess an automatic physiological regulator of sexual activity.

In modern cities, just as in the ruins of antiquity, there appear on the stones of altars and the walls of toilets the drawings of phalluses and vulvas. Priapus in permanent erection and Astarte in panting, eternal heat accompany humankind in all its peregrinations and adventures. Hence we have had to invent rules that channel the sexual instinct and protect society from its overflow. In all societies there exists a series of prohibitions or taboos—and also of stimuli or incentives—whose purpose is to regulate and control the sexual instinct. These rules serve society (culture) and reproduction (nature) at the same time. Without them the family would disintegrate and with it all of society. The human race, subjected to the perpetual electrical discharge of sex, has invented a lightning rod: eroticism. An ambiguous invention, like all the others we have conceived, its vague outline now comes into better focus: it is repression and license, it is sublimation and perversion. And the primal function of sexuality—

reproduction—is subordinated to other ends, some of them social and some of them individual. Eroticism protects society from onslaughts of sexuality but it also negates the reproductive function. It is the capricious servant of life and death.

THE RULES AND institutions meant to tame sex are numerous, ever-changing, and contradictory. It is pointless to list them; they range from the incest taboo to the marriage contract, from obligatory chastity to legislation regulating brothels. Their changes defy any attempt at classification that is anything more than a mere catalog: a new practice appears every day, and every day an old practice disappears. But all are comprised of two terms: abstinence and license. Neither of which is an absolute. This is explainable: the psychic health of society and the stability of its institutions depend in large part on the contradictory dialogue between the two. Since earliest times societies have gone through periods of chastity or continence followed by periods of licentiousness. An example from close at hand: Lent and Carnival. Antiquity and the Orient were also acquainted with this double rhythm: the bacchanal, the orgy, the public penitence of the Aztecs, the Christian processions of amends, the Ramadan of the Muslims. In a secular society such as ours, the periods of chastity and license, almost all of them associated with the religious calendar, are disappearing as collective practices hallowed by tradition. This is of no import: the dual nature of eroticism is preserved intact. No longer a religious and cyclical commandment, it turns into a rule to be followed on an individual level. This rule almost always has an ethical foundation, although it sometimes appeals to the authority of science and hygiene. The fear of disease is no less powerful than the fear of divinity or the respect for moral law. The double face of eroticism—fascination with both life and death—appears once again, divested now of its religious aura. The meaning of the erotic metaphor is ambiguous—or, rather, it is plural. It says many things, all different, but in all of them two words figure: pleasure and death.

In some cases—an exception within the great exception that eroticism represents in the animal world—abstinence and license are not relative and periodic but absolute. These are the extremes of eroticism, and otherworldly. I say this because eroticism is essentially desire: a shot fired in the direction of a world beyond. For the ideal of absolute chastity or of absolute license is truly an ideal; it can very seldom, perhaps never, be realized. The chastity of the monk or nun is continually threatened by the lustful images that appear in dreams, by nocturnal emissions; the libertine, for his part, experiences periods of satiety and surfeit, in addition to being subject to insidious attacks of impotence. Some are victims, as they sleep, of the chimerical embrace of incubi and succubi; others are doomed, when awake, to cross the wasteland of insensitivity. Realizable or not, the ideals of absolute chastity and license may be collective or individual. Both types are part of the vital economy of society, although individual extremes tend to be a personal attempt to break social ties, to achieve a liberation from the human condition. I need not dwell on religious orders, communities, and sects that preach absolute chastity in convents, monasteries, ashrams, and other retreats. All religions have such confraternities and brotherhoods. It is more difficult to document the existence of libertine communities. Unlike religious associations, almost always part of a church and therefore publicly recognized, libertine groups usually meet in remote and secret places. Yet it is easy to attest to their reality: they appear in the literature of all eras, both in the East and in the West. They are not only a social fact but also a literary genre; therefore they are doubly real. But collective erotic practices have also assumed religious forms. Consider the phallic cults of the Neolithic, or the bacchanalia and saturnalia of Greco-Roman antiquity. In two notably ascetic religions, Buddhism and Christianity, the union of the sexual and the sacred also plays a role, and a preeminent one. Every great historic religion has given rise, on its margins or at its very heart, to sects, movements, rites, and liturgies in which the flesh and sex are paths to divinity. It could not be otherwise: eroticism is first and foremost a *thirst for otherness*. And the supernatural is the supreme otherness.

Erotic religious practices are surprising both in their variety and in their recurrence. Collective ritual copulation was practiced by the Tantric sects of India, by the Taoists in China, and by the Gnostic Christians of the Mediterranean region. The same is true for communion with semen, a rite shared by the initiates of Tantrism and by the Christian Gnostics who worshiped Barbelus. Many of these erotico-religious movements, inspired by millennial dreams, combined religion, eroticism, and politics. Among them, the Yellow Turbans (Taoists) in China and the Anabaptist followers of John of Leyden in Holland. I emphasize that in all these rituals, with two or three exceptions, reproduction plays no role, or only a negative one. In the case of the Gnostics, one had to ingest semen and menstrual blood in order to be reintegrated into the Great Whole, for the Gnostics believed that this world was the creation of a perverse demiurge. Among the Tantrists and Taoists, though for opposite reasons, the retention of semen was de rigueur. In Hindu Tantrism, semen was offered as a libation. Coitus interruptus almost always formed part of those rituals. Probably this was also the meaning of the Biblical "sin of Onan." In short, in religious eroticism, the sexual process is reversed; there is appropriation of the immense powers of sex to further ends different from or contrary to reproduction.

EROTICISM IS EMBODIED also in two emblematic figures: the ascetic and the libertine. Emblems that are opposed yet move in the same direction: both, rejecting reproduction, are attempts at salvation or personal liberation from a fallen, depraved, incoherent, or unreal world. The same goal impels sects and communities, except that for them salvation is a collective undertaking—they are a society within a society—whereas the ascetic and the libertine are asocial, individuals confronting society or rebelling against it. The cult of chastity, in the West, is an inheritance from Platonism and other philosophies of antiquity that held the immortal soul to be the prisoner of the mortal body.

The belief generally was that someday the soul would return to the empyrean, and the body to formless matter. Contempt for the body, however, does not appear in Judaism, which always exalted the generative power: *increase and multiply* is the first Biblical commandment. Perhaps for this reason, and because it is the religion of the incarnation of God in a human body, Christianity mitigated Platonic dualism with the dogma of the resurrection of the flesh and of "bodies in Glory." But it stopped short of seeing in the body a path to divinity, a belief widely held by other religions and by many heretical sects. Why? Doubtless because of the influence of Neoplatonism on the Church Fathers.

In the Orient the cult of chastity began as a method for attaining longevity: to store up semen was to store up life. The same was true of the sexual fluids of the woman. Each ejaculation and each female orgasm was a loss of vitality. As this belief evolved, chastity became a method of acquiring—through the subjugation of the senses—supernatural powers, and even, in Taoism, immortality. This is the essence of yoga. Despite the differences, chastity fulfills the same function in the East as in the West: it is a test, an exercise that strengthens us spiritually and allows us to make the great leap from the human to the superhuman.

But chastity is only one path among many. The yogin and the ascetic could employ eroticism too to achieve communion with the divinity, ecstasy, liberation, or the conquest of "the unconditioned." Many religious texts, among them a number of great poems, do not hesitate to compare the ecstatic rapture of the mystic and the bliss of union with the divinity to sexual pleasure. The fusion of the sexual and the spiritual is less common in our tradition than in the Oriental one. The Old Testament, however, abounds in erotic stories, many of them tragic and incestuous, and some have inspired memorable texts. Victor Hugo used the story of Ruth to write "Booz endormi," a nocturnal poem in which "the darkness is nuptial." But Hindu texts are more explicit. Jayaveda's famous Sanskrit poem "Gitagovinda," for instance, sings of the adulterous love of the god Krishna (the Dark Lord) and the milkmaid Radha. As in the case of the "Song of Solomon," the religious meaning of the poem is indistinguishable from its profane erotic meaning: they are two aspects of the same reality. The conjunction of the religious and the erotic vision is frequent among the Sufi mystics. Communion with divinity is sometimes compared to a feast between two lovers in which wine flows in abundance. Divine intoxication, erotic ecstasy.

I referred above to the "Song of Solomon," also known as the "Song of Songs." This collection of poems on the theme of profane love, one of the most beautiful erotic works that the poetic word has created, for more than two thousand years has not ceased to nurture the imagination and the sensuality of humanity. The Jewish and Christian traditions have interpreted these poems as an allegory of the relationship between Jehovah and Israel or between Christ and the Church. To this confusion we owe the "Cántico Espiritual" of St. John of the Cross, one of the most intense and mysterious poems of the Western lyric tradition. It is impossible to read the poems of the Spanish mystic as erotic texts only or as religious texts only. They are both, and something else as well, something without which they would not be what they are: poetry. The ambiguity of the poems of St. John of the Cross has met with resistance and errors of interpretation in the modern era. Some critics insist on regarding them as essentially erotic texts; others consider them sacrilegious. I remember how shocked W. H. Auden was on encountering certain images of the "Cántico Espiritual": they seemed to him a vulgar confusion of the spiritual with the carnal.

Auden's response was more Platonic than Christian. We owe to Plato the idea of eroticism as a vital impulse that ascends, rung by rung, to the contemplation of the highest good. This idea contains another: that of the gradual purification of the soul, which at each step moves farther from sexuality until, at the summit of its ascent, it relinquishes it altogether. But what religious experience tells us—especially through the testimony of the mystics—is precisely the opposite: eroticism, which is sexuality transfigured by human imagination, does not disappear; it changes, is continually transformed, but never ceases to be what it was originally, a sexual impulse.

In the figure of the libertine there is no union between religion and eroticism; on the contrary, there is a sharp and clear division. The libertine sees pleasure as an aim that excludes any other. He is almost always passionately opposed to values and beliefs, whether religious or ethical, that subordinate the body to a transcendent purpose. At one of its extremes, libertinism borders on criticism and becomes a philosophy; at the other, it borders on blasphemy, sacrilege, profanation, things that are the reverse of religious devotion. Sade boasted of professing an intransigent philosophical atheism, but in his books passages of irreligious religious fervor abound, and in his life he had to face a number of accusations of sacrilege and impiety, such as those brought against him at his trial in 1772 in Marseilles. André Breton once told me that Sade's atheism was a belief: it could also be said that libertinism is a religion in reverse. The libertine denies the supernatural world with such vehemence that his attacks are a homage and, at times, a consecration. The real difference between the ascetic and the libertine is that the eroticism of the former is a solitary sublimation, one without intermediaries, while the eroticism of the latter is an act that, if it is to be carried out, requires the presence of an accomplice or a victim. The libertine always needs the Other, and this is his damnation: he depends on his object and is the slave of his victim.

LIBERTINISM, AS AN expression of desire and of the exasperated imagination, is timeless. As a philosophy it is relatively modern. The curious evolution of the words *libertinism* and *libertine* helps us understand the no less curious fate of eroticism in the modern era. In Spanish, *libertino* first meant "son of a freedman," and only later did it designate a dissolute person who led a licentious life. In French, during the seventeenth century, the word had a meaning akin to that of *liberal* and *liberality*: generosity, altruism. The libertines were originally poets or, like Cyrano de Bergerac,

philosopher-poets—adventurous spirits, such as Théo-
phile de Viau and Tristan L'Hermite, with a lively
sense of fantasy and driven by a maniacal imagination.
The meaning of frivolity and insouciance associated
with the word *libertinism* is most charmingly expressed
by Madame de Sévigné: "Je suis tellement libertine
quand j'écris, que le premier tour que je prends règne
tout le long de ma lettre" (I am such a libertine when
I write, that the first tack I take is the one I follow
throughout my letter).[1] In the eighteenth century, libertinism became philosophical. The libertine was the
intellectual critical of religion, laws, and customs. The
shift in meaning was imperceptible, and libertine philosophy turned eroticism into moral criticism. This was
the enlightened mask that timeless eroticism assumed
when it reached the modern age. It ceased to be religion
or profanation, associated in both cases with ritual, and
became ideology and opinion. Since then the phallus
and the vulva have turned into sophists and criticize
our customs, ideas, and laws.

The most complete and trenchant expression of libertine philosophy is found in Sade's novels. In them religion is denounced with no less fury than are the soul
and love. This is explainable. For the libertine the ideal
erotic relationship means absolute power over the sexual

object, and an equally absolute indifference toward its fate; while the sexual object is totally complacent toward the desires and caprices of its lord. Hence Sade's libertines demand the perfect obedience of their victims. This condition can never be satisfied; it is a philosophical premise, not a psychological reality. In order to satisfy his desire, the libertine needs to know (and, to him, to know is to feel) that the body he is touching contains a sensibility and a will that are suffering. Libertinism requires a certain autonomy of the victim, since without it the contradictory feeling that we call pleasure/pain is not produced. Sadomasochism, the center and the crown of libertinism, is therefore also its negation. Feeling negates the sovereignty of the libertine by making him depend on the sensibility of the object; it also negates the passivity of the victim. The libertine and his victim become accomplices at the cost of an unusual philosophical defeat: at one and the same time, the indifference of the libertine and the passivity of the victim are compromised. Libertinism, a philosophy of feeling, postulates an impossible lack of feeling: what the ancients called ataraxia. Libertinism is contradictory: it seeks both the death of the Other and his or her resurrection. The punishment is that the Other does not come back to life as a body but as a shade. Everything

that the libertine sees and touches loses reality. His reality depends on the reality of his victim—but he or
she is merely a scream, a gesture that vanishes. The
libertine turns everything he touches into a phantom,
and he himself becomes a shade among shades.

In the history of erotic literature Sade and his followers occupy a unique position. Despite the intense joy
with which they gather together his lugubrious negations, they are descendants of Plato, who always exalted
Being; they are descendants of Lucifer, sons of fallen
light, black light. For the philosophical tradition, Eros
is a divinity that merges darkness with light, matter
with spirit, sex with idea, the here with the there.
Through these philosophers it is black light that speaks,
which is half of eroticism: a partial philosophy. In order
to find more complete visions we must turn not only
to philosophers but also to poets and novelists. Reflect-
ing on Eros and its powers is not the same as expressing
them: expression is the gift of the artist and the poet.
Sade was a prolix and dull writer, the opposite of an
artist; Shakespeare and Stendhal tell us more about
erotic passion and its mystery than do Sade and his
modern disciples as they struggle bitterly to transform
it into a philosophical discourse. The dungeons and
beds of razors of sadomasochism have turned into a

tedious university chair in which the pleasure/pain pair engage in endless arguments. Freud's superiority lies in the fact that he knew how to bring together his experience as a physician and his poetic imagination. A man of science and a tragic poet, he showed us the path leading to an understanding of eroticism: the biological sciences allied with the intuition of the great poets. Eros is solar and nocturnal: everyone is aware of him, but few see him. He was an invisible presence for Psyche, his beloved, for the same reason that the sun is invisible in full daylight: an excess of light. The twofold aspect of Eros, light and dark, crystallizes in an image repeated a thousand times by the poets of the Greek anthology: the lamp in the darkness of the bedroom.

If we wish to know the luminous side of eroticism, its radiant approval of life, we need only look for a moment at one of those figurines of fertility dating from the Neolithic: its sapling slenderness, the plumpness of the hips, the hands that squeeze the little figure's own breasts like fruits, the ecstatic smile. Or, if we are unable to visit the site, at least to see photographs of the immense carved figures of men and women in the Buddhist sanctuary of Karli, in India. Bodies like powerful rivers or like peaceful mountains, images of a nature at last satisfied, caught at that moment of harmony with the world and the self that follows sexual climax. Solar happiness: the world smiles. For how long? The time of a sigh: an eternity. Yes, eroticism detaches itself from sexuality, transforms it, diverts it from its purpose of reproduction; but this detachment is also a return. The couple return to the sexual sea and are rocked in the infinite, gentle movement of its waves. There they recover the innocence of animals. Eroticism is a rhythm: one of its chords is separation, the other is return, the journey back to reconciled nature. The erotic beyond is here, and it is this very moment. All women and all men have lived such moments; it is our share of paradise.

This experience of a primordial reality before eroticism, love, and the ecstasy of contemplatives, this return is neither an escape from death nor a denial of the terrifying aspects of eroticism: it is an attempt to understand them and integrate them into the whole. Not an intellectual understanding but a sensual one: the wisdom of the senses. D. H. Lawrence sought that wisdom all his life. Shortly before his death, as a miraculous recompense, he left in a fascinating poem the testimony of his discovery: the return to the Great Whole is the descent to the depths, to the underground palace of Pluto and Persephone, the girl who each spring returns to the surface of the earth. A return to the place of origin, where death and life embrace:

Reach me a gentian, give me a torch!
let me guide myself with the blue, forked torch of this
flower
down the darker and darker stairs, where blue is darkened on blueness
even where Persephone goes, just now, from the frosted
September
to the sightless realm where darkness is awake upon
the dark
and Persephone herself is but a voice
or a darkness invisible enfolded in the deeper dark
of the arms Plutonic, and pierced with the passion of
dense gloom,
among the splendour of torches of darkness, shedding
darkness on the lost bride and her groom.[2]

---

1. Translation by Helen Lane.

2. D. H. Lawrence, "Bavarian Gentians," *The Complete Poems of D. H. Lawrence*, collected and edited with an introduction and notes by Vivian de Sala and Warren Roberts (New York: The Viking Press, 1964), II, 697.

Eros and Psyche

ONE OF THE first appearances of love, in the strict sense of the word, is the story of Eros and Psyche that Apuleius includes in one of the most entertaining books of Greco-Roman antiquity: *The Golden Ass* (or *Metamorphoses*). Eros, a cruel divinity whose arrows respect neither his mother nor Zeus himself, falls in love with a mortal, Psyche. It is a story, Pierre Grimal says, "directly inspired by Plato's *Phaedrus*: the individual soul (Psyche), the faithful image of the universal soul (Venus), elevates itself progressively, thanks to love (Eros), from the mortal condition to divine immortality." The presence of the soul in a love story is in fact a Platonic echo, as is, I should add, the search for immortality, which Psyche attains upon becoming united with a divinity. But this is an unexpected transformation of Platonism: the narrative is a realistic love story (there is even a cruel mother-in-law, Venus), not the account of a philosophical adventure. I don't know whether those who have dealt with this subject noted what to me is the real novelty of the story: a god, Eros, falls in love with a maiden who personifies the soul, Psyche. I emphasize, first of all, that their love is mutual and returned: neither is an object of contemplation for the other; nor are they rungs on any ladder of contemplation. Eros loves Psyche and Psyche Eros, and very prosaically they end up marrying each other. There are countless stories of gods who fall in love with mortals, but in none of these loves, invariably sensual in nature, does attraction for the soul of the beloved play a role. Apuleius's story presages a vision of love that a thousand years later will change the spiritual history of the West. Another portent: Apuleius had been initiated into the mysteries of Isis, and his book ends with the appearance of the goddess and the redemption of Lucius, who had been turned into an ass as punishment for his impious curiosity. Transgression, punishment, and redemption are all elements of the Western concept of love. It is Goethe's subject in his *Faust*, Part II, and Wagner's in *Tristan and Isolde*, and Nerval's in *Aurelia*.

In Apuleius's tale, young Psyche, punished for her curiosity—or, rather, for being the slave and not the mistress of her desire—must descend to the underground palace of Pluto and Proserpina, the kingdom of the dead but also of roots and seeds: the promise of resurrection. Having passed the test, Psyche returns to the light, and her lover is restored to her: Eros the invisible reveals himself at last. There is another text that ends with a return and can be read as the counterpart of Psyche's journey. I refer to the final pages of Joyce's *Ulysses*. After wandering about the city, the two characters Bloom and Stephen go back to the Ulysses-Bloom house—or, rather, to Ithaca, where Penelope-Molly awaits them. Bloom's wife is all women, or she is woman herself: the perpetual wellspring, the great cunt, the mother mountain, our beginning and our end. On seeing Stephen, a young poet, Molly decides that he will soon be her lover. Molly is not only Penelope but Venus as well, though without poetry and its powers of consecration she is neither a woman nor a goddess. Molly is unlettered, but she knows that she is nothing without language, without the sublime or stupid metaphors of desire. She therefore adorns herself with flirtatious remarks, with popular songs and tunes as if they were necklaces, earrings, and bracelets. Poetry, the loftiest and the most vulgar, is her mirror; on seeing her image, she enters it, dives deep within her being and becomes a wellspring.

Mirrors and springs appear in the history of erotic poetry as symbols of a fall and a resurrection. Like the woman who contemplates herself in them, springs are waters of both perdition and life; to see oneself in those waters, to fall into them and remain afloat, is to be born again. Molly is a wellspring, and she talks in an endless soliloquy that is like the inexhaustible murmur of a fountain. And what does she say? This entire torrent of words is a great yes to life, a yes indifferent to good and evil, a self-regarding, prudent, avid, generous, bounteous, stupid, cosmic yes, a yes of acceptance that in its monotonous flow fuses and confuses past, present, and future, what we were and are and will be, everything and everyone together in a great exclamation like a sea surge that rises, falls, and jumbles all things together in a whole that has no beginning or end:

O and the sea the sea crimson sometimes like fire and the glorious sunsets and the figtrees in the Alameda

gardens yes and all the queer little streets and pink and
blue and yellow houses and the rosegardens and the
jessamine and geraniums and cactuses and Gibraltar as
a girl where I was a Flower of the mountain yes when
I put the rose in my hair like the Andalusian girls used
or shall I wear a red yes and how he kissed me under
the Moorish wall and I thought well as well him as
another and then I asked him with my eyes to ask
again yes and then he asked me would I yes to say yes
my mountain flower and first I put my arms around
him yes and drew him down to me so he could feel
my breasts all perfume yes and his heart was going like
mad and yes I said yes I will Yes.[1]

Molly's great Yes contains all the negations and turns
them into a hymn to undifferentiated life. It is an affirmation of life similar to that of Duchamp's "Rose
Sélavy." A celebration of Eros, not of Psyche. There is
a phrase in Molly's monologue that no woman in love
would have been able to say: "he kissed me under the
Moorish wall and I thought well as well him as another." No, it is not the same with this one or that one.
And that is the borderline that separates love and eroticism. Love is attraction toward a unique person: a body
and a soul. Love is choice; eroticism is acceptance.

Without eroticism—without a visible form that enters by way of the senses—there is no love, but love goes beyond the desired body and seeks the soul in the body and the body in the soul. The whole person.

THE AMATORY FEELING is an exception within that larger exception that eroticism is to sexuality. But it is an exception that appears in all societies and all periods. There is no people or civilization that does not possess poems, songs, legends, or tales in which the anecdote or the plot—the myth, in the original meaning of the word—is the encounter of two persons, their mutual attraction, and the labors and hardships they must overcome to be united. Their encounter requires, in turn, two contradictory conditions: the attraction that the lovers experience must be involuntary, born of a secret and all-powerful magnetism; at the same time, it must be a choice. In love, predestination and choice, objective and subjective, fate and freedom intersect. The realm of love is a space magnetized by encounter.

For a long time I believed, following Denis de Rougemont and his famous book *Love and the Western World*, that this sentiment was exclusive to our civilization and that it was born in a definite place and period: Provence between the eleventh and twelfth centuries. Today this opinion seems untenable to me. First of all, a distinction must be made between the amatory sentiment and the idea of love adopted by a society and a period. The former belongs to all times and places; in its simplest and most immediate form it is the passionate attraction we feel toward one person out of many. The existence of an immense literature whose central subject is love is conclusive evidence of the universality of the amatory sentiment. I emphasize: the sentiment, not the idea. Love in this rudimentary form is a mysterious and passionate attraction toward a single person, that is to say, the transformation of the erotic object into a free and unique subject. Sappho's poems are not a philosophy of love; they are an attestation, the shape in which that strange magnetism has crystallized. The same can be said of the songs collected in the *Shih Ching* (*The Book of Songs*), of many collections of Spanish ballads, or of any other poetic anthology of this sort. But sometimes reflection on love becomes the ideology of a society; then we find ourselves in the presence of a way of life, an art of living and dying, an ethic, an aesthetic, and an etiquette. A *courtesy*, to use the medieval term.

Courtesy is not within the reach of all: it is a body of knowledge and a practice. It is the privilege of what might be called the aristocracy of the heart. Not an aristocracy founded on bloodlines and inherited privileges but on certain qualities of the spirit. Although these qualities are innate, in order that they be manifested and made second nature, the adept must cultivate his mind and his senses, learn to feel, speak, and sometimes remain silent. Courtesy is a school of sensibility and selflessness. "Razón de amor," a beautiful love poem and the first in the Spanish language (thirteenth century), begins as follows:

> Quién triste tiene su corazón
> Venga oír esta razón.
> Oirá razón acabada,
> hecha de amor e bien rimada.
> Un escolar la rimó
> que siempre dueña amó;
> más siempre hubo crianza
> en Alemania y Francia
> moró mucho en Lombardía
> para aprender cortesía. . . .

> (Whoever has reason to lament
> let him come hear this argument.
> He will hear sound reasoning

Filled with love and rhyme's seasoning.

A scholar set it in verse:

To highborn ladies not at all averse,

he was schooled in true romance

in Germany and France;

and long dwelt in Lombardy

to learn courtesy. . . .)[2]

"Courtly love" is learned: it is a knowledge of the senses illuminated by the light of the soul, a sensual attraction refined by courtesy. Analogous forms of this flourished in the Islamic world, in India, and in the Far East. There too a culture of love existed, the privilege of a small, select group of men and women. Persian and Arabic literatures, both closely associated with court life, are rich in poems, stories, and treatises on love. And there are two great novels, one Chinese and the other Japanese, that are essentially stories of love, both taking place in a closed and aristocratic milieu.

Ts'ao Hsúeh-ch'in's *Dream of the Red Chamber* (*Hung Lou Meng*) takes place in a palatial mansion, and the hero and two heroines belong to the aristocracy.[3] The book is augmented by poems and reflections on love. These latter are a mixture of the metaphysics of Buddhism and of Taoism, the whole tinged with popular beliefs and superstitions, as in the *Tragicomedia de Calixto y Melibea*, Spain's great and awesome book of love. Confucius's stern philosophy scarcely appears in *The Dream of the Red Chamber*, except as a tedious set of prohibitions and precepts with which adults attempt to thwart youth—hypocritical rules behind which those same adults conceal their own cupidity and lust. Opposition between the profane and the sacred world: the morality of Bao-yu and Dai-yu's elders is mundane, whereas the love of the two young people is the fulfillment of a destiny decreed thousands of years before. *The Tale of Genji* (*Genji Monogatari*), by Murasaki Shikubu, a lady of the Japanese court, is similar: the characters are members of the highest nobility, and their love is seen from the viewpoint of a melancholy philosophy steeped in Buddhism and the sense of the impermanence of the things of this world. It is odd that Denis de Rougemont ignored this evidence that wherever a high courtly culture flourishes, a philosophy of love springs forth. That philosophy is to emotion in general as emotion is to eroticism and the interconnections of both with sexuality. The image of concentric circles, evoked at the beginning of these pages, appears again: sex is the root, eroticism the stem, and love the flower. And the fruit? The fruits of love are intangible. This is one of love's mysteries.

ONCE THE EXISTENCE of ideologies of love in other civilizations has been accepted, I can add that there are fundamental differences between them and the ideology of the West. The principal difference, it seems to me, is that in the East love was conceived of within a religious tradition; it was not an independent thought but a derivative of some doctrine. In the West, from the beginning, the philosophy of love lay outside official religion and at times was in opposition to it. Plato's reflection on love is inseparable from his philosophy, and that philosophy abounds in criticisms of myths and religious practices (for example, of prayer and sacrifice as a means of securing favors from the gods). Courtly love was viewed by the Church not only with alarm but also with censure. No such thing is to be found in the Oriental tradition. Ts'ao Hsúeh-ch'in's novel is composed as a counterpoint between two worlds which, although separate, are in communication with each other: the beyond of Buddhism and Taoism, peopled by monks, ascetics, and divinities, and the passions, encounters, and separations of a polygamous aristocratic family in eighteenth-century China. Religious metaphysics and psychological realism. The same duality governs Lady Murasaki's novel. None of these works, or other novels, works for the theater, and poems whose theme was love, were accused of heterodoxy. Some were criticized and at times even forbidden because of their daring and their obscenities, but not because of their ideas.

The Occidental conception of fate and its reverse and complement, freedom, is substantially different from the Oriental. This difference includes two other ideas that are closely associated: the responsibility of each one of us for our acts, and the existence of the soul. Buddhism, Taoism, and Hinduism share the belief in metempsychosis, although the notion of an individual soul is not very clear in their various doctrines. For Hindus and Taoists what we call the soul is but a moment within a reality that has been changing unceasingly from what it was in the past and that will continue to change in lives to come, until final liberation is attained. As for Buddhism, it categorically denies the existence of an individual soul. In the two novels—to return to the works of Ts'ao Hsúeh-ch'in and Lady Murasaki—love is a fate imposed by the past. More precisely, it is the karma of each character. Karma, as is well known, is simply the result of our previous lives. Hence the sudden love of Yugao for Genji and the jealousy that he arouses in the "lady of Rokujo" are the fruit not only of his present life but, more, of his lives before. Shuichi Kato notes how often Lady Murasaki uses the word *shukuse* (karma) to explain the behavior and the fate of her characters. On the other hand, love in the West is a fate freely chosen: by that I mean, no matter how powerful the influence of predestination—the best-known example is the magic potion that Tristan and Isolde drink—in order for their destiny to be fulfilled, the cooperation of the lovers is necessary. Love is an indissoluble knot that ties together fate and freedom.

I now point to a similarity that in the end turns into a new opposition. In *The Dream of the Red Chamber* and *The Tale of Genji*, love is a school for disillusionment, a path on which the reality of passion is little by little revealed to be a chimera. As in the Western tradition, death has the function of awakening the lover lost in dreams. In both works the analysis of the passion of love and its real and unreal nature is penetrating and astute: hence they have been compared with a number of European novels and in particular with Proust's. *À la recherche du temps perdu* is the story of a long sinuous peregrination that leads the narrator from one disillusionment to another. Guided by that Virgil who goes by the name of involuntary memory, he reaches the contemplation of the reality of realities: time itself. In the two Oriental novels the path of disillusionment does not lead to the salvation of the ego but to the revelation of an emptiness—ineffable and inexpressible. We see not an appearance of something but a disappearance: that of our own selves. At the end of Proust's work the narrator contemplates the crystallization of lived time, a time that is his alone and nontransferable, and yet it is no longer his: it is reality such as it truly is, scarcely more than a vibration, our share of immortality. Proust's journey is a personal search inspired by a philosophy that is independent of an official religion; the searches of the protagonists of Ts'ao Hsúeh-ch'in and Lady Murasaki are a confirmation of the truths and teachings of Buddhism and Taoism. In the Orient, love, however violent its transgressions, was lived and reflected on within religion; it could constitute a sin but not a heresy. In the West, love developed outside religion and even in opposition to it. Occidental love is the offspring of philosophy and of the poetic sentiment that transfigures into an image everything it touches. Thus for us love has been a *cult*.

It is not surprising that the philosophy of love first

appeared in Greece. Philosophy there became separate from religion very early: Greek thought began with the pre-Socratic philosophers' critique of myths. If the Hebrew prophets criticized society from the point of view of religion, Greek thinkers criticized the gods from the point of view of rational thought. Nor is it surprising that the first philosopher of love, Plato, was also a poet: the history of poetry is inseparable from that of love. Plato's influence has been a lasting one, and continues even today, above all because of his idea of the soul; without it our philosophy of love would not exist or would have had a very different form, one hard to imagine. The idea of the soul, according to the experts, is not Greek. In Homer the souls of the dead are not truly souls, incorporeal entities; they are shades. For an ancient Greek the distinction between the body and the soul was not clear-cut. The idea of a soul different from the body first appears in certain pre-Socratics such as Pythagoras and Empedocles; Plato adopts it, systematizes it, makes it one of his fundamental concepts, and bequeaths it to his successors. But it is not the same soul that appears later in Provence, in Dante, in Petrarch. Plato's idea of love is not the same as ours. It can even be said that his is not really a philosophy of love but, rather, a sublimated (and sublime) form of eroticism.

This statement may seem rash, but it is not. Read the two dialogues devoted to love, the *Phaedrus* and the *Symposium*, the latter in particular, and compare them with the other great works on the same subject that have been handed down to us by philosophy and poetry.

The *Symposium* is made up of various discourses on or eulogies of love delivered by seven guests. In all likelihood they represent the opinions and the points of view on the subject that were current in that era, except for the discourse of Socrates, which expresses Plato's own ideas. The splendid speech by Aristophanes is particularly memorable. To explain the mystery of the universal attraction that individuals feel toward each other, he refers to the myth of the original androgyne. Once upon a time there were three sexes: the male, female, and androgynous, and they were so strong and intelligent that they represented a threat to the gods. To subjugate them, Zeus decided to split each in two. Ever since then, the separate halves wander, each searching for its complementary half. The myth of the androgyne is not only profound but also awakens in us profound resonances: we are incomplete beings, and the desire for love is a perpetual thirst for completion. Without my male or female other I will not be myself. This myth and that of Eve, who is born from Adam's rib, are

poetic metaphors that, without really explaining anything, say much about love. But they are not a philosophy, answering the mystery of love with another
question. Moreover, the myth of the androgyne does
not touch upon certain aspects of the love relation that
to me are essential, such as the tie between freedom and
predestination or between mortality and immortality.

The centerpiece of the *Symposium* is the discourse of
Socrates. The philosopher tells his listeners of a conversation he had with a wise foreign priestess, Diotima
of Mantineia. Plato often uses ancient (or invented)
myths set forth by an illustrious visitor. It seems odd
that, in a predominantly homosexual group such as the
circle surrounding Plato, Socrates should present a doctrine of love from the mouth of a woman. I am of the
opinion that it is a question of a *recollection*, in the
precise meaning that Plato gives this word: a descent to
the origins, to the kingdom of the mothers, the place
of primal truths. Nothing is more natural than to make
an old prophetess the one who reveals the mysteries of
love. Diotima begins by saying that Eros is neither god
nor man; he is a *daemon*, a spirit whose life is lived
between gods and mortals. The preposition *between* defines him: his mission is to communicate, and to unite
living beings. Perhaps that is why we confuse him with

the wind and represent him with wings. He is the child of Poverty and Abundance, and this explains his nature as an intermediary: he links light with darkness, the world of the senses with the world of ideas. As the child of Abundance, he distributes worldly goods. It is the one who desires who petitions, the one who is desired who gives.

Love is not beautiful: it desires beauty. All men desire. This desire is a search for the possession of what is best. The strategist desires to be victorious, the poet to compose a hymn of insuperable beauty, the potter to fashion perfect amphoras, the tradesman to accumulate goods and money. And what does the lover desire? He seeks human beauty. Love is born the moment one sees a beautiful person. Even though desire is universal and spurs everyone on, each desires something different. When Diotima reaches this point, she warns Socrates: Love is not simple. It is a mixture of several elements united and animated by desire. Nor is its object simple. Love is something more than the attraction of human beauty, which is subject to time, death, and corruption. Diotima goes on: All men desire the best, beginning with what they do not have. We are content with our body if its members are sound and agile; but if our legs were deformed and refused to support us, we would not hesitate to exchange them for those of a champion runner. Likewise with everything we desire. And what is the benefit to us when we obtain what we desire? The objects vary but the benefit is the same: we feel happy. Men aspire to happiness and want it to last forever. Love's desire for beauty is also the desire for happiness, not a perishable happiness of the moment but a perpetual happiness. All men suffer from a lack: their days are numbered, they are mortal. The aspiration to immortality is a trait that unites and defines all men.

The desire for the best, then, is allied to the desire to possess and enjoy it forever. All living beings, not only humans, share this desire: to perpetuate themselves. The desire for reproduction is one of the elements of love. There are two kinds of reproduction: by way of the body and by way of the soul. Men and women, enamored of each other's beauty, join their bodies together to reproduce themselves. Procreation, Plato says, is divine, among animals and humans alike. But the other mode of procreation is higher, for the soul engenders in another soul imperishable ideas and feelings. Those who are "fecund by way of the soul" conceive through thought: poets, artists, sages, and also the creators of laws and those who teach moderation and justice to their fellow citizens. A lover can thus engender, in the soul of his beloved, knowledge, virtue, and veneration of what is beautiful, just, and good. Diotima's discourse and the comments by Socrates are a sort of pilgrimage. As we go on, we discover new aspects of love, like the person who, on climbing a hill, contemplates with each step the changes of the view that lies below. But there is a part that we cannot see with our eyes, only with our understanding. "All that I have revealed to you," Diotima tells Socrates, "are the minor mysteries of love." She then proceeds to instruct him in the loftiest and the most deeply hidden mysteries.

In our youth we are attracted by corporeal beauty, and we love only one body, one beautiful form. But if what we love is beauty, why love it only in one body and not in many? And Diotima asks again: If beauty exists in many forms and persons, why not love it in and of itself? And why not go beyond the forms and love the thing that makes them beautiful, the idea? Diotima sees love as a ladder: at the bottom, love of a beautiful body; then the beauty of many bodies; after that, beauty itself; after that, the virtuous soul; and, finally, incorporeal beauty. If love of beauty is inseparable from the desire for immortality, why not participate in it through the contemplation of the eternal forms?

Beauty, truth, and virtue are three and one; they are facets of the same reality, the only real reality. Diotima concludes: "He who has followed the path of love's initiation in the proper order will on arriving at the end suddenly perceive a marvelous beauty, the source of all our efforts. . . . An eternal beauty, nonengendered, incorruptible, that neither increases nor decreases." A beauty that is entire, one, identical to itself, that is not made up of parts as the body is or of ratiocinations, as is discourse. Love is the way, the ascent, toward that beauty: it goes from the love of one body to the love of many, then from the love of all beautiful forms to the love of virtuous deeds, then from deeds to ideas and from ideas to absolute beauty, which is the highest life that can be lived, for in it "the eyes of the understanding commune with beauty, and man engenders neither images nor simulacra of beauty but beautiful realities." And this is the path of immortality.

DIOTIMA'S DISCOURSE IS sublime. And Socrates is worthy of it because of his life and, above all, because of his death. To comment on this discourse is like interrupting the silent contemplation of the sage with the idle talk and squabbles of the world here below. But that same love of truth—even though in my case it is

limited and not at all sublime—obliges me to ask myself: Did Diotima really speak of love? She and Socrates
spoke of Eros, that *daemon* or spirit personifying an
impulse that is neither purely animal nor purely spiritual. Eros can lead us astray, make us fall into the
swamp of concupiscence and the pit of the libertine; it
can also ennoble and raise us to the loftiest contemplation. This is what I have called *eroticism* throughout
these reflections and what I have endeavored to distinguish from love properly speaking. I repeat: I speak of
love as we know it from Provence. This love, although
it existed in a diffuse form as a sentiment, was not
known to ancient Greece either as an idea or as a myth.
Whereas erotic attraction toward a unique person is
universal and appears in all societies, the idea or philosophy of love is historical and arises only where certain social, intellectual, and moral circumstances are
present. Plato would doubtless have been shocked at
what we call love. Some of its manifestations, such as
the idealization of adultery, suicide, and death, would
have repelled him; others, such as the worship of
woman, would have amazed him. And sublime loves,
such as Dante's for Beatrice or Petrarch's for Laura,
would have struck him as a sickness of the soul.

The *Symposium* also contains ideas that would shock

us if it were not for the fact that we read them at a
certain historical distance. For example, when Diotima
describes the rungs of the ladder, she says that a lover
begins by loving only one beautiful body, but that it is
absurd not to recognize that other bodies are beautiful,
absurd not to love them all. It is clear that Diotima is
speaking of something very different from what we call
love. For us fidelity is one of the conditions of the love
relationship. Diotima seems to know nothing of fidelity,
and it never even occurs to her to give thought to the
feelings of the man or woman we love: she sees the
beloved as a mere step on the ascent toward contemplation. In reality, love for Plato is not strictly speaking
a relationship; it is a solitary adventure. Reading certain
passages of the *Symposium*, it is impossible not to think,
despite the sublimity of the concepts, of a philosophical
Don Juan. The difference is that the course taken by
the Seducer of Seville leads downward and ends in hell,
whereas that of the Platonic lover culminates in the
contemplation of the Idea. Don Juan is subversive, inspired more by false pride and the temptation to defy
God than by the love of women. This is the reverse
image of Plato's eros.

The severe condemnation of physical pleasure and
the preaching of chastity as the path to virtue and bliss

are the natural consequence of the Platonic separation of body and soul. For us that separation is too categorical. This is one of the traits that characterize the modern era: the boundary between the soul and the body has become less well defined. Many of our contemporaries no longer believe in the soul, a concept rarely used by modern psychology and biology. At the same time, what we call *body* is much more complex today than it was for Plato. Our body possesses attributes that previously belonged to the soul. The punishment of the libertine, as I attempted to show above, lies in the fact that the body of his victim, the erotic object, is also a consciousness; through that consciousness the object is transformed into a subject. The same can be said of the Platonic conception. For Plato erotic objects—whether they be the body or the soul of the ephebe—are never subjects: they have a body and do not feel, they have a soul and remain silent. They are really *objects*, and their function is that of being stages in the ascent of the philosopher toward the contemplation of essences. Although in the course of this ascent the lover—or, rather, the master—has relations with other men, his path is essentially a solitary one. In his relationship with others there can be a dialectic, that is to say, a division of discourse into parts, but there is no true dialogue or conversation. The text of the *Symposium*, although it takes the form of a dialogue, is made up of seven separate discourses. In the *Symposium*, eroticism in its purest and loftiest expression, the necessary condition of love—the other man or woman who accepts or refuses, who says yes or no and whose very silence is an answer—does not appear. The Other, who is the lover's complement, the man or woman who turns the lover's desire into mutual choice, into free will, into freedom.

---

1. James Joyce, *Ulysses* (New York: The Modern Library, 1942), 768.
2. Translation by Helen Lane.
3. Although the title of the novel, *The Dream of the Red Chamber*, is a beautiful one and has been hallowed by the authority of the years, it is incorrect. *Hung Lou Meng* actually means *Dream of Red Mansions*. The houses of the rich were called that because of the red color of their walls; the houses of commoners were gray.

The Prehistory of Love

ON BEGINNING THESE reflections, I pointed out the affinities between eroticism and poetry: the first a metaphor of sexuality, the second an eroticization of language. The relationship between love and poetry is even more intimate. First lyric poetry and then the novel—which is poetry after its own fashion—have been vehicles of the amorous sentiment. What poets, dramatists, and novelists have told us about love is no less precious and profound than the meditations of the philosophers. And frequently it is closer to the truth, closer to human and psychological reality. Platonic lovers, such as the *Symposium* describes them, are few. The emotions which Sappho traces in a few lines on contemplating a beloved are anything but Platonic:

> My tongue sticks to my dry mouth,
> Thin fire spreads beneath my skin,
> My eyes cannot see and my aching ears
> Roar in their labyrinths.
>
> Chill sweat slides down my body,
> I shake, I turn greener than grass.
> I am neither living nor dead and cry
> From the narrow between.[1]

It is not easy to find in Greek poetry poems that match this intensity, but there are any number of compositions with a similar theme, except that they are not lesbian. In this regard, too, Sappho was an exception: feminine homosexuality, unlike the masculine, rarely appears in Greek literature. The border between eroticism and love is a shifting one, but it does not strike me as too rash a statement to assert that the great majority of Greek poems are more erotic than they are amorous. This applies also to the *Palatine Anthology*. Some of its brief poems are unforgettable: those of Meleager, several attributed to Plato, some by Philodemus, and, in the Byzantine period, those of Paulus Silentiarius. In all of them we see, and hear, the lovers in their different moods—desire, sensual pleasure, disillusionment, jealousy, ephemeral happiness—but never the sentiments and emotions of the Other. Nor are there dialogues of love—in the manner of Shakespeare or Lope de Vega —in the Greek theater. Aegisthus and Clytemnestra are united by crime, not by love: they are accomplices, not lovers. Phaedra is devoured by solitary passion and Medea by solitary jealousy. To find prefigurations of what love was to be for us, we must go to Alexandria and Rome. Love is born in metropolises.

The first great love poem is a work by Theocritus: "The Sorceress."[2] It was written in the first quarter of the third century B.C. and today, more than two thousand years later, even when read in translations which no matter how good they are remain translations, it preserves its force of passion intact. The poem is a long monologue by Simaetha, Delphis's abandoned lover. It begins with an invocation to the moon in its three manifestations: Artemis, Selene, and Hecate the terrible. Then follows the discontinuous story told by Simaetha as she gives orders to her maidservant to execute this or that part of the black rite of which both women are devotees. Each magic spell is marked by a pointed refrain: "Magic bird, bring me back my lover, bring him to my house."[3] As the servant spreads a little burned flour on the floor, Simaetha says that it is "the bones of Delphis." As she burns a branch of laurel that crackles and is consumed, leaving almost no ashes, she calls down a curse upon her faithless lover: "May his flesh thus burn. . . ." After offering three libations to Hecate, she throws into the fire a strip of the cloak Delphis inadvertently left behind in her house and bursts out: "Why, cruel Eros, have you stuck to my flesh like a leech? Why do you suck my black blood?" When she has finished her imprecation, Simaetha bids her acolyte to scatter herbs on Delphis's threshold and spit on them, saying: "I crush your bones." But as Simaetha incants, confessions and complaints escape her lips: she is possessed by desire, and the fire that she kindles to burn her lover is the fire by which she herself is being consumed. Rancor and love conjoined: Delphis deflowered and abandoned her, but she cannot live without the man she hates. It is the first time that there appears in literature—and described, furthermore, with such violence and force—one of the great human mysteries: the inextricable commingling of hate and love, spite and desire.

Simaetha's amorous frenzy appears to be inspired by Pan, the sex god with the hoofs of a male goat, whose running makes the forest tremble and whose breath shakes the foliage and makes females delirious. Pure sexuality. But once the rite is performed, Simaetha grows calm, as beneath the moon the surging tide of the sea abates and the wind in the grove dies down. Then she entrusts herself to Selene as to a mother. Her story is a simple one. From what she recounts we learn that she is a free woman of modest estate (although not wretchedly poor: she has a servant); that she lives alone (she speaks of women friends and neighbors but not of her family); and that she has an occupation of some sort, perhaps to support herself. She is a commoner, a young woman such as exist by the thousands in every city of the world, ever since there have been cities: today Simaetha could live in New York, Buenos Aires, or Prague. One day neighboring women invite her to a procession in honor of Artemis. A flirt, she dresses in her best garments and covers her shoulders with a linen shawl that a friend lends her. Among the crowd she meets two young men who have just left the palestra, men with tanned, gleaming torsos and blond beards. A *coup de foudre*: "I saw . . ." Simaetha says, but does not say who it was she saw. Why? She has seen reality itself

in a body and a name: Delphis. She returns home, per-
turbed, obsessed. She suffers from fever and sleepless-
ness for days on end. She consults wizards and witches,
as today we consult psychiatrists, and like us with no
result. She suffers from

> the pangs of love, which only worsen
> unless he himself appears in person.

Not without misgivings—she is chaste and proud—she
sends Delphis a message. The young athlete immediately presents himself at her house, and Simaetha, on
seeing him, describes her emotion in almost the same
turns of phrase as Sappho: "I was bathed in an icy sweat
from head to foot. . . . I was unable to say a word, not
even those stammers with which little children call out
to their mothers in their sleep; and my body, incapable
of movement, was that of a wax doll."[4] Delphis wears
himself out making promises and that very day shares
her bed with her. This meeting is followed by many
others. Suddenly an absence of two weeks, and the in-
evitable gossip passed on by a friend: Delphis has fallen
in love with another—although, the indiscreet tale-
bearer says, she doesn't know whether it is with a man
or a woman. Simaetha ends with a vow and a threat:

she loves Delphis and will seek him out, but should he reject her, she has poisons that will kill him. And she takes her leave of Selene (and of us): "Farewell, serene goddess: I will endure my misfortune as I have until now; farewell, goddess with the resplendent face, farewell, stars that accompany your chariot in its slow journey through the calm of night." Simaetha's love is made of persistent desire, despair, anger, helplessness. We are very far from Plato. Between what we desire and what we value there is a gap: we love what we do not value and we desire to be forever with a person who makes us unhappy. In love, evil makes its appearance: it is a pernicious seduction that attracts us and overcomes us. But which of us dares condemn Simaetha?

THEOCRITUS'S POEM COULD not have been written in the Athens of Plato. Not just because of Athenian misogyny, but because of the situation of women in Greece in the classical period. In the Alexandrian period, which bears more than one resemblance to our own, an invisible revolution takes place: women, shut up in the gynaeceum, come out into the open air and appear on the surface of society. Some of them were famous, not in literature and the arts but in politics—

Olympias, for instance, the mother of Alexander and Arsinoë and the wife of Ptolemy Philadelphus. This change was not limited to the aristocracy but extended to the immense and boisterous population of tradesmen, craftsmen, small property owners, hirelings, and all those people in large cities who have lived and live still on very little money. Apart from its literary value, Theocritus's poem indirectly sheds light on Hellenistic society. To a certain extent it is a poem of mores, showing us not the life of princes and potentates but that of the city's middle class with its passions great and petty, its difficulties, common sense, and madness. Through this poem and others of his, as well as through the "mimes" of Herodas, we have some notion of the status of women and their relative freedom.

To make a poor young woman like Simaetha the focus of a poem of passion that alternately moves us and makes us smile was an immense literary and historical innovation. The literary innovation we owe to Theocritus and his genius; the historical, to the society in which he lived, to the social change that in turn was a consequence of the great creation of the Hellenistic period—the transformation of the city of antiquity. The polis, closed in upon itself and jealous of its autonomy, opened outward. The great cities turned into genuine cosmopolises through the interchange of persons, ideas, mores, and beliefs. Among the Hellenistic poets represented in the *Palatine Anthology* a number were foreigners, such as Meleager the Syrian. This great civilizing creation was achieved amid the wars and tyrannies that mark the period. The most dramatic novelty must have been the appearance, in the new cities, of a freer woman. The erotic object beginning to transform itself into a subject. The prehistory of love in the West lies, as I have said, in two great cities: Alexandria and Rome.

Women—more precisely, patrician women—occupy an outstanding place in the history of Rome, during both the Republic and the Empire. Mothers, wives, sisters, daughters, lovers: there is no episode in Roman history in which a woman did not stand at the side of an orator, warrior, politician, or emperor. Some were heroic, some virtuous, some infamous. In the last years of the Republic another social category made its appearance: the courtesan. She soon became one of the centers of worldly life and an object of scandal. Both patricians and courtesans were free women in several senses of the word: by their birth, their means, and their mores. Free above all because to an unprecedented degree they had the freedom to accept or reject their lovers. They were the mistresses of their bodies and their souls. The heroines of erotic and amorous poetry come from both classes.

As in Alexandria, young poets formed groups that gained notoriety from their works, opinions, and love affairs. Catullus was one of these. His literary quarrels and satires were no less famous than his love poems. He died young. His best poems are in the form of a confession of his love for Lesbia, a poetic name that hid the identity of a patrician known for her beauty, position, and dissolute life (Clodia). A love story alternately happy and unhappy, naive and cynical. The union of opposites—desire and contempt, sensuality and hatred, paradise glimpsed and hell endured—is achieved in brief poems of great intensity. Catullus's models were the Alexandrian poets, above all Callimachus—famous in antiquity, yet only fragments of his work survive— and Sappho. Catullus's poetry has a unique place in the history of love because of the economy of means with which he expresses what is most complex: the simultaneous presence in the same consciousness of hatred and love, desire and contempt. Our flesh covets what our reason condemns.

Catullus's conflict is similar to Simaetha's, though there are important differences. The first of them is sex: in his poems it is a man who speaks. It is the man, not the woman, who is in a situation of dependency. The second: the hero is not a fictional character and he speaks in his own name. By this I do not mean to say that Catullus's poems are simply confessions or confidences; in them, as in all literary works, there is a fictitious element. The poet who speaks is and is not Catullus: he is a *person*, a mask that allows the poet's real face to be seen and yet at the same time conceals it. His sorrows are real, but they are also figures of speech. They are images, representations. The poet turns his love into a sort of novel in verse, though it is a novel actually lived and suffered. Another difference: both lover and beloved belong to the upper classes. Since they are socially independent beings—she because of her position, he because he is a poet—they dare to violate the conventions and rules that restrict them. Their love is an exercise in freedom, a transgression, a defiance of society. This is a theme that will occur more and more frequently in the annals of amorous passion, from Tristan and Isolde to the novels of our own day. Finally, Catullus is a poet, and his realm is that of the imagination. Unlike Simaetha, who is simpler and cruder, he does not try to exact vengeance with philters and poisons; his vengeance takes an imaginary form— his poems.

Three elements of modern love make their appearance in Catullus: choice—the freedom of the lovers; defiance—love is a transgression; and jealousy. Catullus expresses in lucid and moving poems the power of a passion that little by little filters into our heart until it paralyzes our will. He was the first to warn of the chimerical nature of jealousy and its powerful psychological reality. It is impossible to confuse this jealousy with the feeling of sullied honor. In Othello jealousy—he loves Desdemona—is mingled with the wrath of a man whose honor has been offended. But love, in the perverted form of jealousy, is the passion that drives him: "And I will kill thee, / And love thee after." On the other hand, the characters in Spanish dramas, particularly those of Calderón, are not jealous: when they take their revenge, they are removing a blot on their honor, almost always one that is imaginary. They are not in love; they are the guardians of their reputation, the slaves of public opinion. As one of them says:

> The despotic legislator
> has placed my reputation
> in another's hand and not in mine.

In all these examples, the social code is the deciding factor. Not in Proust, however, the great modern poet not of love but of its poisonous secretion, its fatal pearl: jealousy. Swann knows that he is the victim of a delirium. Neither the tyranny of sexual attraction nor that of the spirit binds him to Odette. Years later, recalling his passion, he confesses to himself: "And to think that I wasted the best years of my life for a woman who wasn't my type." His attraction to Odette is an inexplicable sentiment, except in negative terms: Odette fascinates him because she is inaccessible—not her body, her mind. Like the ideal beloved of the Provençal poets, she is unattainable. Despite the ease with which she surrenders herself, she forever eludes him by the mere fact that she exists. Odette is unfaithful and lies continually, but even if she were true to him and sincere, she would still elude him. Swann can touch and possess her, isolate her, lock her up, turn her into his slave: a part of her will always elude him. Odette will always be *other*. Does Odette really exist, or is she her lover's fiction? Swann's suffering is real, but is the woman who causes it real as well? Yes, she is a presence, a face, a body, an odor, and a past that will never be his. An impenetrable presence: what is there behind those eyes, that mouth, those breasts? Swann will never know. Perhaps not even Odette knows; she lies not only to her lover but to herself.

Odette's mystery is that of Albertine and Gilberte: the Other always escapes us. Proust endlessly analyzes his unhappiness, obsessively dissects Odette's lies and Albertine's subterfuges, refusing to recognize the freedom of the Other. Love is the desire to possess; it is also a detachment. In Proust it is exclusively the former, and for that reason his vision of love is negative. Swann suffers, sacrifices himself for Odette, ends up marrying her and giving her his name. Did he ever love her? I doubt it, and he too doubts it. Catullus and Lesbia are asocial; Swann and Odette amoral. She does not love him; she uses him. He does not love her either; he holds her in contempt. Nonetheless he cannot tear himself away from her; his jealousy ties him to her. He is enamored of his suffering, and his suffering is pointless. We live with phantoms, and we ourselves are phantoms. There are only two ways out of this imaginary prison. The first is the path of eroticism, and we have already seen that it ends in a blind wall. The question of the jealous lover—What are you thinking about? What are you feeling?—has no answer except sado-masochism: tormenting the Other or tormenting himself. In either case the Other is inaccessible and invulnerable. But we are not transparent, either, for others or for ourselves. This constitutes humanity's original sin, the brand that marks us from birth. The other way out is that of love: surrender of self, acceptance of the freedom of the beloved. Madness, an illusion? Perhaps, but it is the only door that leads out of the prison of jealousy. Many years ago I wrote: Love is a sacrifice without virtue. Today I would say: Love is a bet, a wild one, placed on freedom. Not my own; the freedom of the Other.

THE AUGUSTAN AGE is that of great Latin poetry: Virgil, Horace, Ovid. All of them have bequeathed us memorable works. But love poems? Those of Horace and Ovid are variations, often perfect ones, on the traditional themes of eroticism, almost always steeped in Epicureanism. And what about Virgil? St. Augustine said: "I wept for Dido when I ought to have wept for my sins." Great praise of an unsurpassable artist—yet the description of the love of Aeneas and Dido is grandiose in the manner of an opera or a tremendous storm seen from afar: we admire it, but it does not touch us. A far more imperfect poet, Propertius, was able to communicate with greater immediacy the sorrows and joys of love. Propertius invents a heroine: Cynthia. She is both literary figure and real person. We know that she existed and we know her name, Hostia, though scholars argue as to whether she was a courtesan or a woman married to a man of means. A novelistic love affair, but quite real: meetings, separations, infidelities, lies, surrenders, endless quarrels, moments of sensuality, passion, anger, morose melancholy.

Propertius's modernity is extraordinary. I shall add that it is the modernity of Rome. Not a great city—*the* city. Many of the incidents and episodes related in certain elegies could have been taken from a modern novel or film. For instance: Cynthia takes a stroll on the outskirts of Rome with a man friend, ostensibly to honor chaste Juno, though in reality it is Venus she is honoring. Propertius decides to avenge himself and organizes a little spree in an isolated spot. As he endeavors to divert himself with two courtesans he has met in dubious surroundings—the picture is completed by an Egyptian flutist and a dwarf who claps his hands to the music—Cynthia suddenly bursts upon the scene, disheveled and furious. A pitched battle, scratching and biting, the flight of the two courtesans, and the neighborhood in an uproar. Cynthia wins, and in the end forgives her lover (IV, 8). Realism, love of the picturesque, and detail that is true to life, passionate, and grotesque. Humor that spares neither the author nor his beloved. Ezra Pound rediscovered that humor and appropriated it. But Propertius's modernity is not merely literary; it is a link in the history of amorous poetry.

One of Propertius's elegies inaugurates a poetic mode destined to have illustrious successors. I am referring to the seventh elegy in Book IV. Certain critics condemn it; they are of the opinion that it is in bad taste, both because of its subject and because of some turns of phrase. For my part, I find it deeply disturbing. The poem begins with the statement of an unusual fact, which the poet sets forth as though it were something natural and within the normal order of things: "It is not a fable, the Manes exist; the shade of the dead escapes the funeral pyre and returns to our midst." Cynthia has died and been cremated only the day before. The place where cremations take place is by a noisy thoroughfare and thus reminiscent of a cemetery in Paris or New York. At precisely the hour that her lover remembers her, her ghost presents itself in his solitary bed. She is the same as always—beautiful, though a little pale. There are appalling details: part of her tunic is scorched, and the aquamarine she once wore on her ring finger has disappeared, devoured by the flames of the funeral fire. Cynthia has returned to reproach him for his infidelities— she forgets, as usual, her own—to remind him of his betrayals, and to tell him once again of her love for him. The ghost's communication with him ends with these words: "You may now keep company with other women, but soon you will be mine, mine alone." There is a hallucinatory contrast between the supernatural nature of the episode and the realism of the description, a realism emphasized by Cynthia's attitude and her words, her complaints, her jealousy, her erotic transports, the scorched tunic, the ring that is missing. Cynthia relives her passion as though she had not died: she is a true soul in purgatory. At the end of their mournful meeting, she flees the arms of her lover—not of her own will but because dawn is breaking "and an inescapable law orders shades to return to the waters of the Lethe." Once again she says to him: "You will be mine, and I shall mix the dust of your bones with the dust of mine" (*Mecum eris et mixtis ossibus ossa teram*). Sixteen hundred years later Quevedo was to write: "They will be dust, but dust in love" (*Polvo serán mas polvo enamorado*).

Although the literature of antiquity is full of ghosts, none of those apparitions has the terrifyingly physical reality of Cynthia's specter. Nor her funereal eroticism: compelled by divine law, Cynthia leaves the arms of her lover against her will, and this separation is equiv-

alent to a second death. Ulysses and Aeneas descend to
the realm of shades and speak with the dead: one of
them makes the journey in search of Tiresias to learn
what destiny awaits him, and the other goes in search
of his father, Anchises. Both are surrounded by throngs
of illustrious dead: kinfolk, friends, heroes and heroines.
In none of these meetings is there a trace of eroticism.
Aeneas spies Dido among the shades—like one, Virgil
says, "who sees or believes he sees the moon feebly
pierce the clouds"—but the queen, out of spite, does
not answer his words of repentance and withdraws into
the depths of the forest. The scene is a moving one, yet
the emotion it arouses in us belongs to another category
of feeling: compassion. Cynthia's visit, on the other
hand, is an amorous meeting of a live man and a dead
woman. Propertius begins a genre that will come down
through time to Baudelaire and his descendants: the
erotic encounter with the dead. The Middle Ages were
populated by incubi and succubi, demons that in the
form of a man or a woman slipped into the beds of
friars and virgins, of servants and their mistresses, and
copulated with them. These lascivious apparitions and
the "demon of middle-age love"—who tempts the sons
of Saturn, those belonging to religious orders and re-
cluses cultivating the life of the spirit—are different

from Cynthia's ghost. They are infernal spirits, not souls of the dead.

In the Renaissance and Baroque periods visits by ghosts are associated with Neoplatonism. The most impressive example is Quevedo's sonnet: "Amor constante más allá de la muerte" (Love faithful beyond death). A black-and-white star, burning hot and ice cold. In accord with Platonic doctrine, at the hour of death the immortal soul abandons the body and ascends to the higher spheres or else returns to the earth to purge itself of its faults. The body rots and again becomes amorphous matter; the souls of lovers seek each other and are united. In this respect Christianity coincides with Platonism, for even the souls of adulterers Paolo and Francesca revolve together in the second circle of hell. But there is a substantial difference: contrary to Platonic doctrine, Christianity saves the body, which after the Last Judgment comes back to life in the eternity of Glory or Avernus. Quevedo breaks with this twofold tradition and says something that is neither Platonic nor Christian. His sonnet has been universally and justly admired, but in my opinion its unusualness has not been noticed, nor all the things that separate it from the Neoplatonic. This is not the occasion to undertake an analysis of this poem, and my commentary will be brief. For greater clarity I give the text:

"AMOR CONSTANTE MÁS ALLÁ DE LA MUERTE"

Cerrar podrá mis ojos la postrera
Sombra que me llevare el blanco día,
Y podrá desatar esta alma mía
Hora, a su afán ansiosa lisonjera;

Mas no de esotra parte en la ribera
Dejará la memoria, en donde ardía;
Nadar sabe mi llama el agua fría,
Y perder el respeto a la ley severa.

Alma, a quien todo un Dios prisión ha sido,
Venas, que humor a tanto fuego han dado,
Médulas, que han gloriosamente ardido:

Su cuerpo dejarán, no su cuidado:
Serán ceniza, más tendrán sentido;
Polvo serán, mas polvo enamorado.

(The final shadow may close my eyes,
carry me off from white of day,
unchaining my soul at the hour
of its anxious obsequious desire:

but it will not leave the memory
of that other shore where once it burned:
for my fire can swim me through the frigid water,
irregardless of the strictures of law.

A soul which once imprisoned an entire God,

veins that brought fuel to such flames,

marrow that so gloriously burned:

they'll leave this body, but not its cares:

ash they'll be, yet still aware;

they will be dust, but dust in love.[5]

In the first quatrain the poet evokes—or, more exactly, convokes—the day of his death. The visible world vanishes, and the soul, unchained from time and its deceptions, returns to the nocturnal darkness of the beginning, which is also that of the end. Conformity with the law of life: men are mortal, and their hours are numbered. In the second quatrain conformity turns into rebellion. An unusual and scarcely Christian transgression: the memory of his love will continue to burn on the other shore of the Lethe. The soul, burning with passion and becoming a swimming flame, crosses the river of oblivion. The conjunction of fire and water is a metaphor as old as the human imagination, which from the very beginning was bent on bringing the opposition of the elements into unity. In Quevedo's sonnet the nuptials of fire and water assume a relationship to polemical and complementary time. The flame battles the water and overcomes it; the water in turn is an obstacle that at the same time allows the flame to float on its moving surface. The soul, a flame in love, violates the "strictures of law" that separate the world of the dead from the world of the living.

The first tercet consummates the transgression and makes way for the final metamorphosis. Swiftly enumerating, Quevedo unites, without confusing them, the soul and the body, the latter personified by two elements of the erotic passion: blood and marrow. The first verse says that the soul has lived a prisoner of "an entire God." Not the Christian God but one god among others, though a great one: Eros, love. The image of love as a prison appears in other poems by Quevedo: for example, the sonnet that has as its subject a portrait of his beloved that he wore in a ring: "In a small cell I bear imprisoned . . ." In general, and as we see precisely in this sonnet, the prisoner is not the soul of the lover but the figure of the beloved, who is engraved (imprisoned) in the heart or in the soul of her lover. The lover, Sor Juana says in another sonnet, fashions in his imagination a prison in which to confine the image of the beloved. Although Quevedo says the opposite—the soul of the lover is the prisoner—this does not efface the relationship between the two terms of lover and beloved. In any event, in both cases the symbol of the couple is the desire that devises an amatory prison. Desire is a consecration, either because the prison is divine (Eros) or because the prisoner is a goddess or a semigoddess (the beloved woman). One of the key notions of love in the Western world is thus preserved: the consecration of the beloved. In its two aspects the image suggests Holy Communion, a disturbing and sacrilegious analogy which is a violation of Platonism and Christianity alike. The second line takes up once again the conjunction between water and fire but now in a more pronounced and violent way: the body's blood feeds the immaterial flame of passion. The third line is no less impressive: the fire of passion consumes the marrow of the bones. Another fusion of the material and the spiritual: the marrow is the most intimate and secret part of the person, "the most substantial part," the dictionary says, "of an immaterial thing."

The surprising final tercet is the result of the transmutation that is the amorous battle between fire and water, life and death. In the first line the soul of the lover abandons his body but not the body's concerns. An affirmation of the immortality of the soul, though it is still caught up in the snares of this world. The soul continues to be bound, by desire, to another body, that of the beloved woman. The "care" that the soul retains on the shore of the river of forgetfulness, and that turns memory into a swimming flame, is not the love of eternal ideas or the Christian God: it is desire felt for a human, mortal person. Blake's phrase "eternity is enamored of the works of time" is perfectly applicable to this blasphemous verse. The following line inverts the terms of the paradox: the veins will be ashes, "yet still aware." The inanimate remains of the body will lose neither sensibility nor consciousness; they will feel and they will be aware of their feeling. The marrow is the object of the same transmutation: although it will be dust, base matter, it will go on loving. The remains of the dead lover, without ceasing to be a material residue, will retain the attributes of the soul and of life: feeling and meaning. In the Platonic tradition, the soul abandons the body in search of the eternal Forms; in the Christian tradition, the soul will be reunited with its body someday—the day of days (the Last Judgment). An heir to both traditions, Quevedo alters them, and to some degree profanes them: although the body deteriorates into formless matter, that matter is animate. The power that animates it and imbues it with a terrible eternity is love, desire.

Religion and poetry live in continual osmosis. In Quevedo's sonnet the myths and the rites of Greco-Roman paganism are present; the mysteries of Christianity are also present, though in a less direct way. The theme of the sonnet is profoundly religious and philosophical: the survival of the soul. But Quevedo's vision is unique and, in its uniqueness, tragic. The body will cease to be a human form; it will be lifeless matter but go on loving nonetheless. The distinction between soul and body vanishes. Defeat of the soul: everything returns to dust. Defeat of the body: that dust is animate and feels. Fire, destroying the body, also animates it and turns it into ashes that desire. The fire of the poem is a metaphor for passion; in the mind of the reader, however, it suggests the pagan Greco-Roman rite of cremation frowned upon by the Church. It is impossible to know whether Quevedo was aware of this association; in all likelihood he allowed himself to be carried away by unconscious images. But this is not important; what matters is what the reader feels on reading the poem—and what the reader feels is that the fire of love soon ceases to be a worn-out metaphor and becomes a real flame that devours the body of the dead person. The resurrection of an image that lies in the collective unconscious of our civilization. The *Diccionario de Au-*

toridades, defining the word *ceniza*, says that it means "the bones and remains of the deceased, alluding to the custom introduced and observed by antiquity of burning the bodies of the dead and preserving their ashes in tombs, urns, or pyramids." Quevedo's sonnet is an urn in the form of a pyramid, a flame.

In the modern era the meeting with the dead takes other forms. Some of them are suffused with religiosity and see in the visit of the dead beloved a promise of redemption: Nerval's Aurelia, Novalis's Sophie. At other times the vision presents itself as a guilty hallucination, or as the projection of a perverse consciousness. In Baudelaire's visions evil triumphs, with a cortege of vampires and demons. It is not easy to determine if such images come from a sick mind or are a form of remorse. The theme of the erotic ghost in modern literature is widespread—this is not the time to explore it, nor do I feel capable of doing so. I remember only a poem by López Velarde which combines the religious promise of salvation through love, a favorite theme of the Romantics, with the realism of Propertius. Written shortly before the poet died, it remained unfinished and contains two indecipherable verses. Which makes it even more impressive.

The poem creates a mood admirably conveyed by

one of López Velarde's favorite words: *zozobra* (anxiety). It is an account of a dream that the poet calls apocalyptic, and can be read as a double premonition: of his last years and of a funereal wedding. The dream expresses his desires and fears: a love poem to a dead woman and terror in the face of death. López Velarde could have said, as Nerval did: "C'est la mort—ou la morte?" (Is it death—or the dead woman?) His vision is realistic. Although he does not mention her by name, it is clear that the ghost is Fuensanta, the beloved of his youth to whom he dedicated his first book. Having died a few years before, in 1917, she was buried in the Valley of Mexico, far from her native province. For that reason he calls her "the prisoner of the Valley of Mexico." He also mentions the dress in which she was buried, bought on a vacation trip. The ghost, wearing a pair of black gloves, draws him "to the ocean of her breast." A chilling correspondence between the two poems: Propertius recounts that despite the fact that the voice and the appearance of Cynthia's ghost were those of a living being, "the bones of her fingers creaked when she moved her frail hands"; López Velarde, less grimly, says that their four hands intertwined "as if they were the four foundations of the construction of the universe" and asks himself:

Did you preserve your flesh in each bone?
The mystery of love was hidden completely
in the prudence of your black gloves.

The poems by Catullus and Propertius are somber visions of love: jealousy, betrayals, abandonment, death. But just as in the face of Sade's black eroticism we have Lawrence's solar passion and Molly Bloom's great Yes of acceptance, so in Greco-Roman literature there are poems and novels that celebrate the triumph of love. I have already mentioned Apuleius's tale. Another example is the pastoral romance *Daphnis and Chloë*, the little masterpiece by Longus. The Greek novels of the Alexandrian and Roman period abound in amorous episodes. Few people read them today, but in their time they were immensely popular, as widely read as romantic novels are now. They were read also in the sixteenth and seventeenth centuries. Cervantes confesses that the work of his old age, *Los trabajos de Persiles y Segismunda* (*The Trials of Persiles and Segismunda*), which he regarded as his most perfect and best-written novel, was inspired by Heliodorus. Modern criticism adds another Greek influence: Achilles Tatius. Authors as different as Tasso, Shakespeare, and Calderón admired Heliodorus and sometimes imitated him. We know the love that Racine professed as an adolescent for Theagenes and Charicleia, the main characters of Heliodorus's romance *Aethiopica*. Surprised by his stern teacher in the midst of reading that profane author, Racine endured without complaint the book's confiscation, saying: "It doesn't matter, I know it by heart." People's fondness for this sort of reading matter was explainable: apart from recounting reversals of fortune and adventures that were very entertaining, it showed the readers of the sixteenth and seventeenth centuries an aspect of antiquity quite different from that of the classical era, closer to their own preoccupations and sensibility. Unlike the Latin novels, such as *The Satyricon* and *The Golden Ass*, which really belong to the picaresque genre, the principal subject of the Greek novels was love.

The preeminence of erotic subjects—primarily heterosexual—is characteristic of the literature and art of the Hellenistic era. Michael Grant points out that one of the most famous poets of the time, Apollonius of Rhodes, "was the first to make love a cardinal subject of epic poetry."[6] The story of Medea's passion for Jason is referred to in *The Argonautica*. That love had been a tragic subject for Euripides; Apollonius turned it into a romantic story. In New Comedy the focus of the dramatic action is invariably the love of a young man of good family for a hetaera or slave girl who in the end turns out to be the daughter of a prominent citizen, stolen at birth. The heroines of Euripides were queens and princesses; those of Menander, daughters of bourgeois families. Women of humble station, like Theocritus's Simaetha also abound in these works, or women brought low by cruel fortune. The hetaeras, who had enjoyed a prestigious position in the Athens of Pericles, continued to do so in Alexandria and the other cities. In the novels of Heliodorus, Tatius, and others, the heroes are princes and princesses reduced to servitude, slavery, and other misfortunes by a capricious Fortune that has replaced Fate. Their complicated and fantastic adventures—imprisonment, escape, skirmishes, tricks to deceive despots in rut and queens in heat—have as their background and accompaniment shipwrecks, the traversing of deserts and mountains, and travels through barbarous lands with strange customs. Exoticism has always been one of the seasonings of love stories. But travel served another function: that of obstacle to overcome. The journey separated the lovers but in the end, unexpectedly, united them. After a thousand hardships, free finally of the malevolence and lust of male and female tyrants, the lovers return to their native land safe, sound, and chaste, in order at last to marry each other.

Classical society frowned on amorous passion. In *Phaedrus*, Plato considers it a delirium. Later, in the *Laws*, he went so far as to proscribe even homosexual love. The other philosophers were no less severe, and even Epicurus saw in love a threat—to the serenity of the soul. But the Alexandrian poets exalted it, though without closing their eyes to the havoc it wrought. I have already suggested historical, social, and spiritual reasons for this great change. In the large urban centers a new type of man and woman appeared, who were their own masters. The twilight of the democracies and the rise of powerful monarchies caused a general retreat to private life. Political freedom was replaced by inner freedom. In this shift of ideas and customs, the new situation of women was a decisive factor. We know that for the first time in Greek history women began to engage in occupations and serve functions outside their homes. Some were magistrates, a thing that would have been unheard of for Plato and Aristotle; some were midwives; and some devoted themselves to philosophical studies, painting, poetry. Married women were quite free, as can be seen from the vulgar language of the gossips in Theocritus and Herodas. Marriage began to be seen as a matter that ought not to be arranged by the heads of families alone, but as an agreement in which the participation of the contracting parties was essential. All of which shows, yet again, that the emergence of love is inseparable from the emergence of woman. There is no love without feminine freedom.

An Athenian of the fifth century B.C. was, above all, a citizen; an Alexandrian of the third century B.C. was a subject of Ptolemy Philadelphus. "The Greek novel, New Comedy, and later, the amatory elegy," Pierre Grimal says,[7] "could not be born except in a society that had loosened traditional ties so as to give the individual a greater place. . . . The novel opens the doors of the gynaeceum and leaps over the walls of the garden in which the daughters of decent families strolled." This was possible because an intimate space of freedom had been created, a space opened to the gaze of the poet and the public. The private individual appears, and with him a new freedom: "Tradition puts the tragic hero in chains and decides his fate, whereas the hero of the novel is free." Political duties, extolled by the philosophy of Plato and Aristotle, are moved to the sidelines of society by the search for personal happiness, wisdom, or serenity. Pyrrho seeks indifference; Epicurus temperance; Zeno impassibility: private virtues. Others, such as Callimachus and Meleager, seek pleasure. All of them scorn political life.

In Rome the elegiac poets boast that they serve a militia different from the one that does battle in times of civil strife or conquers distant lands for Rome: they are enrolled in the *militia amoris*. Tibullus praises the Golden Age because, contrary to his own, "which has bloodied the seas and brought death everywhere," it was unacquainted with the scourge of war: "The cruel art of the warrior had not yet forged the sword." The only battles that Tibullus glorifies in his poems are those of love. Propertius is more defiant. In an elegy, he leaves to Virgil the glory of celebrating the victory of Augustus at Actium; he prefers to sing of his amorous relations with Cynthia, like "voluptuous Catullus, who with his verse made Lesbia more famous than Helen." In another elegy he breezily tells us how he feels about patriotic deeds: "The divine Caesar [Augustus] is making ready to take his arms to the Indus . . . to control the currents of the Tigris and the Euphrates . . . to bring to the temple of Jupiter the trophies of the vanquished Parthians. . . . I for my part am satisfied to applaud the parade from the Via Sacra." All these testimonials from Alexandria and Rome belong to what we have called the *prehistory* of love. They extol a passion that classical philosophy condemned as an enslavement. The attitude of Propertius, Tibullus, and other poets was a defiance of society and its laws, an authentic precursor of what today we call civil disobedience. Not in the name of a general principle, as in the case of Thoreau, but because of an individual passion, as with the hero of *L'âge d'or*, the film by Buñuel and Dali. The poets could have said also that love is born of an involuntary attraction that our free will transforms into a voluntary union. Voluntary union is love's necessary condition, the act that turns bondage into freedom.

---

1. Guy Davenport, *Archilochos. Sappho. Alkman* (Berkeley: University of California Press, 1980), 85.

2. Or "The Witches." According to Marguerite Yourcenar, the literal translation is "The Magic Philters" (*Pharmaceutria*). Another translator, Jack Lindsay, sensibly prefers to use as a title the name of the heroine, Simaetha.

3. Magic bird: an instrument used in witchcraft, composed of a metal disk with two perforations and made to rotate by means of a cord. It referred to the wryneck, the bird into which a nymph, the procuress of the adultery of Zeus with Io, was transformed by Hera.

4. Catullus also imitated, almost word for word, the same passage from Sappho—yet another example of how the most intimate and personal poetry is compounded of imitation and invention.

5. Translation by Eliot Weinberger. See my book *Convergences* (New York: Harcourt Brace Jovanovich, 1987), 236.

6. Michael Grant, *From Alexander to Cleopatra: The Hellenistic World* (New York: Macmillan, 1982).

7. Pierre Grimal, introduction to *Romans grecs et latins* (Paris: Bibliothèque de la Pléiade, Gallimard, 1958).

The Lady and the Saint

GRECO-ROMAN ANTIQUITY knew love, almost always, as a passion that was painful but nonetheless worthy of being experienced, desirable in and of itself. This truth, a legacy of the poets of Alexandria and Rome, has lost nothing of its validity: love is desire for *completeness* and therefore answers a profound human need. The myth of the androgyne is a psychological reality: all of us, men and women alike, seek our lost half. But the ancient world lacked a doctrine of love, a set of ideas, practices, and behaviors embodied in and shared by a collectivity. The theory that could have fulfilled that function, the Platonic eros, instead deprived love of its true nature, turning it into a philosophical-contemplative eroticism from which, moreover, women were excluded. In the twelfth century, in France, love makes its appearance at last, no longer an individual delirium, an exception or aberration, but a superior ideal of life. "Courtly love" has something miraculous about it, since it was not a result of religious sermonizing or any philosophical doctrine. It was the creation of a group of poets within a rather restricted society: the feudal nobility of the south of ancient Gaul. It was not born in a great empire, nor was it the fruit of an old civilization: it arose among a group of semi-independent noble domains, in a period of political instability but immense spiritual fecundity. It was an annunciation, a springtime. The twelfth century was the century of the birth of Europe, and in it emerged what later would be the great creations of our civilization—among them lyric poetry and the idea of love as a way of life. It was the poets who invented courtly love. ("Provençal poetry" is a misnomer, from both the linguistic point of view and the geographic, but a misnomer hallowed by tradition.)

The literature on courtly love is vast. I will touch on only a few points that I consider essential to these reflections. I have dealt with this subject in other texts, and with two other subjects that are closely related: love in the poetry of Dante and love in the lyric poetry of the Spanish Baroque. In this essay I will not return to that material.[1] The term *courtly love* reflects the medieval distinction between *court* and *town*. Not vulgar love—copulation and procreation—but a lofty sentiment, characteristic of a noble court. The poets did not call it courtly love; they used another expression, *fin' amors*, that is to say, purified, refined love. A love that did not have as its aim either carnal pleasure or reproduction. An asceticism and an aesthetic. Although there were notable figures among these poets—Guilhem IX de Poitiers, Duke of Aquitaine (the first Provençal poet), Jaufre Rudel, Marcabru, Bernart de Ventadour, Arnaut Daniel, Bertran de Born, the Countess of Die (Beatriz or Isoarda?), Peire Vidal, Peire Cardenal— their collective work is of more importance. Individual differences, though profound, were no impediment to the sharing of the same values and the same doctrine. In less than two centuries these poets created a code of love, many aspects of which are still valid, and bequeathed to us the basic forms of Western lyric verse. In Provençal poetry love between a man and a woman is usually the subject; and the poems are written in the vernacular. In *La Vita Nuova*, Dante offers a reason for this preference of the vernacular over Latin: the poets wished to be understood by the ladies of the court. Poems not to be read but heard, accompanied by music, in the court of the castle of a great lord. This happy combination between spoken word and music could come about only in a society inclined toward refined pleasures, a society made up of men and women of the nobility. And therein resides a great historical innovation: the Platonic banquet had been for men only, and the gatherings hinted at in the poems of Catullus and Propertius had been lively parties of libertines, courtesans, and free-living ladies like Clodia.

Various circumstances made the birth of courtly love possible. First, the existence of relatively independent and rich feudal domains. The twelfth century was a period of affluence: a flourishing cultivation of crops, the beginnings of an urban economy, trade not only between the various regions of Europe but also with the Orient. It was a period that opened outward: thanks to the Crusades, Europeans had closer contact with the Middle East, with its riches and its sciences; through Arabic culture they rediscovered Aristotle, Greco-Roman medicine and science. A number of the Provençal poets took part in the Crusades. The founder of the Provençal school, William of Aquitaine, had been to Syria and Spain. The relations with the latter were particularly fruitful in the realms of politics, commerce, and customs. It was not unusual to find Arab singers and dancers from Al Andalus (areas in Spain held by the Moors) in the courts of feudal lords. At the beginning of the twelfth century the south of France was a privileged place where the most diverse influences were interwoven, from Nordic to Middle Eastern. This diversity bore abundant fruit, producing an extraordinary culture that it is no exaggeration to call the first European civilization.

The appearance of courtly love would have been impossible without the change in the status of women. The women of the aristocracy in particular enjoyed greater freedom than their grandmothers had in the Dark Ages. Several circumstances favored this development. One was religious in nature: Christianity had endowed women with a dignity unknown in the days of paganism. Another was the Germanic heritage: Tacitus had long before noted with surprise that Germanic women were much freer than Roman ones (*De Germania*). Finally, the condition of the feudal world. Marriage between members of the nobility was based not on love but political, economic, and strategic interests.

In that world constantly at war, war at times in distant lands, long absences were frequent, and feudal lords had to leave the governing of their realms to their wives. Marital fidelity was not strict, and examples of extramarital relations abound. Around this time the Arthurian legend of the adultery between Queen Guinevere and Lancelot was popular, as well as the sad fate of Tristan and Isolde, the victims of a guilt-ridden passion. The ladies in question, moreover, belonged to powerful families, and some of them warred with their spouses openly. William of Aquitaine had to endure being abandoned by his second wife, who, taking refuge in an abbey[2] and forming close ties with a bishop, did not cease her efforts against her husband until she had had him excommunicated. Among the women of this period the figure of Eleanor of Aquitaine stands out: the wife of two kings, the mother of Richard the Lion-Hearted, and patroness of poets. A number of ladies of the aristocracy were also troubadors, including the Countess of Die, a famous *trobairitz*. Women enjoyed freedoms in the feudal period that through the combined action of the Church and the absolute monarchy they later lost. The phenomenon of Alexandria and Rome was repeated: the history of love is inseparable from the history of the freedom of women.

It is not an easy task to determine what ideas and doctrines exerted an influence on courtly love. In any case, they were few in number. Provençal poetry was born in a profoundly Christian society, yet on many essential points courtly love departs from the teachings of the Church or is even their opposite. The education, culture, and beliefs of the poets were Christian, but many of their ideals and aspirations were in conflict with Roman Catholicism. They were true believers, and at the same time they assumed an active role in a secular cult that was not that of Rome. This contradiction apparently did not trouble them, at least in the beginning, but it did not go unnoticed by the Church authorities, who disapproved of courtly love. As for the influence of Greco-Roman antiquity, it was of little importance. The Provençal poets were acquainted with the Latin poets in a vague and fragmentary way. There was admittedly the precedent of a "neo-Latin" literature, the product of men of the cloth who wrote "amatory epistles" in the manner of Ovid; but according to René Nelli "they had no influence either on the style of the first troubadours or on their ideas concerning love."[3] Several critics maintain that the prosody of Latin liturgical poetry influenced the metrics and strophic forms of Provençal lyric verse. This is possible, though the religious subjects of that poetry could not have influenced the erotic songs of the Provençal troubadours. Finally: Platonism, the great erotic and spiritual ferment of the Western world. Although there was no direct transmission of the Platonic doctrines on love, it is likely that certain reflections of those ideas reached the Provençal poets through the Arabs. This hypothesis merits a separate comment.

DISCUSSING THE CONNECTION between Arabic "courtesy" and that of southern France, René Nelli says: "The earliest, most profound, and most decisive influence was that of Muslim Spain. The crusades in Spain taught the barons of the South more than did the crusades in the Middle East." The majority of specialists in this field agree that the Provençal poets adopted two popular Arabic-Andalusian poetic forms: the *zajal* and the *jarcha*. Another borrowing that had a great influence not only on the poetry but also on the customs and beliefs: the reversal of the positions of the lover and his lady. The main axis of power in feudal society was the vertical link, both juridical and sacred, between lord and vassal. In Muslim Spain the emirs and the great lords had declared themselves to be the servants, the slaves of their beloveds. The Provençal poet adopted this Arab custom, reversed the traditional relationship of the sexes, called his lady his mistress and himself her servant. In a society much more open than the Hispano-Muslim one—a society in which women enjoyed liberties unthinkable under Islamic rule—this change was a real revolution. It upset the images of man and woman hallowed by tradition, affected mores, left its mark on vocabulary, and through language influenced the vision of the world. Following the usage of the poets of Al Andalus, who called their beloved *sayyidí* (my master) and *mawlanga* (my owner), the Provençal poets called their ladies *midons* (*meus dominus*: my ruler). It is a usage that has come down to our own day. The masculinization of the role of women emphasized the shift in the hierarchy of the sexes: the woman now occupied the superior position, and the lover was her vassal. Love is subversive.

We can now take up the thorny subject of Platonism. In Arabic eroticism the highest love is the purest: all the writers of treatises on love extol continence and chastity. This idea did originate with Plato, although it underwent modifications by Islamic theologians. The influence of Greek philosophy on Arabic thought is well known. The *falasifos* (the Arabic transcription of the word *philosophers*) had access at an early date to the works of Aristotle and certain Platonic and Neoplatonic texts. There is a line of Arabic philosophers whose thought is suffused with Neoplatonism. It is useful to distinguish between those who conceived of love as a path to divinity and those who limited it to the human sphere, though with a window opening onto the higher sphere. For Islamic orthodoxy the mystic way that seeks union with God is a heresy: the distance between the Creator and the creature is insurmountable. Despite this prohibition, one of the spiritual riches of Islam is Sufi mysticism, which fully accepts the path that leads to union with God. A number of Sufi poets and mystics were martyred for their ideas. Mohammed Ibn Dàwud, a jurist and poet of Baghdad, was a follower of the orthodox school. His case is unusual, for he was also the author of a book, *Kitab-al-Zahra* (*The Book of the Flower*), that is a treatise on love in which the influence of the *Symposium* and the *Phaedrus* is clearly perceptible: love is born at the sight of a beautiful body, the steps of love ascend from the physical to the spiritual, the beauty of the male beloved is a way to the contemplation of the eternal forms. But Ibn Dàwud, faithful to orthodoxy, rejects union with God: divinity, sempiternal otherness, is inaccessible.

A century later, in the Córdoba of the Omayyads,

philosopher and poet Ibn Hazm, one of the most attractive figures of Al Andalus, wrote a short treatise on love, *The Necklace of the Dove*, today translated into nearly every European language. Those of us who read Spanish have the great good fortune of having the admirable version of Emilio García Gómez.[4] For Ibn Hazm, as for Plato, love is born from the sight of physical beauty. He also speaks, though in a less systematic way, of the ladder of love that goes from the physical to the spiritual. Ibn Hazm mentions a passage from Ibn Dàwud, which in turn is a quotation from the *Symposium*: "My opinion [on the nature of love] is that it consists of the union between the parts of souls that go about divided, by comparison with how they were at the beginning in their elevated essence, but not as Ibn Dàwud (may God have pity on him!) asserts when, basing himself on the opinion of a certain philosopher, says that souls are 'spheres divided in two,' save for the relationship that they had previously in their highest world. . . ." The philosopher is Plato, and the "divided spheres" are a reference to the discourse on androgynes in the *Symposium*. The idea that souls seek each other in this world because of the relationship they had before descending to earth and assuming a body can also be traced to Plato: it is the doctrine of *reminiscence*.

There are other echoes of the *Phaedrus* in *The Neck-lace of the Dove*. "I see a human form, but when I meditate more thoroughly, I think I see in it a body that comes from the celestial world of the Spheres." Contemplation of beauty is an epiphany. And I have found another echo of Ibn Hazm, not in the Provençal poets but in Dante. In the first chapter of *The Necklace of the Dove* we read: "Love, in and of itself, is an accident and therefore cannot be the basis of other accidents" (Chapter 1: "The Essence of Love"). In Chapter XXV of Dante's *La Vita Nuova* it is stated in almost the same words: "Love does not exist in and of itself as a substance: it is the accident of a substance." In either case the meaning is clear: love is neither an angel (an intelligent incorporeal substance) nor a human being (an intelligent corporeal substance) but *something that happens* to people: a passion, an accident. The distinction between substance and accident is more Aristotelian than Platonic, but what I wish to emphasize is the odd coincidence between Ibn Hazm and Dante. I believe that, with the passage of the years, the idea of Asín Palacios, the first to discover the presence of Arabic thought in Dante's poetry, is meeting with more and more confirmation.

Were the Provençal poets acquainted with Ibn

Hazm's treatise? Even though it is impossible to be certain, there are indications of the influence of this Arabic work on *fin' amors*. More than one hundred and fifty years later, André le Chapelain (Andreas Capellanus) writes, at the request of Marie of Champagne, the daughter of Eleanor of Aquitaine, a treatise on love, *De arte honesta amandi*, in which he repeats ideas and formulas that figure in *The Necklace of the Dove*.[5] It is not unwarranted to suppose, moreover, that before André le Chapelain's treatise was written (1185), poets became acquainted, even if in a fragmentary way, with the ideas of Arabic eroticism at the same time that they assimilated the metrical forms and amatory vocabulary of Arabic poetry. There are numerous affinities: the cult of physical beauty, the rungs of the ladder of love, the praise of chastity—a method for the purification of desire and not an end in itself—and the vision of love as the revelation of a transhuman reality, but not as a way to reach God. This last point is crucial: neither courtly love nor Ibn Hazm's eroticism is a mysticism. In both, love is human, exclusively human, although it contains reflections of other realities or, as Hazm puts it, of the "world of the Spheres." My conclusion: the Western concept of love shows a greater affinity with that of the Arabs and Persians than with those of India and the

Far East. This is not surprising: both the Western and Arabic concepts are derivations—or, more exactly, departures—from a monotheistic religion, and both share the belief in a personal, eternal soul.

COURTLY LOVE FLOURISHED in the same period and in the same geographical region in which the Cathar heresy appeared and spread.[6] Owing to its egalitarian preachings and the purity and upright conduct of its bishops, Catharism quickly gained a vast popular audience. Its theology impressed scholars, the bourgeoisie, and the nobility. Its criticisms of the Roman Church encouraged a populace weary of the abuses of the clergy and the intrusion of papal legates. The ambition of the great overlords, who coveted the wealth of the Church and felt threatened by the French monarchy, also favored the new faith, as did a collective feeling which I hesitate to label nationalistic: the pride and the awareness of sharing a language, customs, a culture. It was a vague yet powerful feeling: that of belonging to a community, Occitania, the country of the *langue d'oc*, a rival of the *langue d'oïl*. Two societies, two sensibilities that had crystallized around two ways of pronouncing the word *oui*, which defines us not by what we deny but by what we affirm and what we are.

The Cathar religion, taking root in Occitania, became identified with the language and the culture of that region. Many of the great lords and ladies who were patrons of the troubadours were sympathetic to the doctrine. Although there were few Cathar troubadours— and none of them wrote amorous poetry—it is natural that there should be some affinity between courtly love and the beliefs of the Cathars. Denis de Rougemont went further: he believed that the Provençal poets had been inspired by the Cathar doctrine and that their fundamental ideas came from it. From one deduction to another he reached the conclusion that love in the West was a heresy—a heresy unaware that it was a heresy. De Rougement's idea is tempting, and I confess that for a while it convinced me. I no longer agree with it, and will now explain why.

More than a heresy, Catharism was a religion, since its fundamental belief was a dualism opposed to the Christian faith in all its versions from Roman Catholicism to the Byzantine Church. It originated in Persia, the cradle of dualistic religions. The Cathars professed not only the coexistence of two principles—light and darkness—but, at the most extreme, the coexistence of two creations, an Albigensian idea. Like a number of Gnostic sects of the centuries immediately after Christ, the Cathars believed that the earth was the creation of a perverse demiurge (Satan) and that matter, in and of itself, was evil. They also believed in the transmigration of souls, condemned violence, were vegetarians, preached chastity (reproduction was a sin), did not condemn suicide, and divided the members of their church into "those who were Perfect" and mere believers. The growth of the Cathar Church in the south of France and the north of Italy is an amazing phenomenon, but not without an explanation: dualism is a natural response to the horrors of this world. God cannot be the creator of a world subject to the accidental, to time, to pain and death; only a demon could have created an earth steeped in blood and ruled by injustice.

But none of these beliefs has any connection with courtly love. The contrary, rather, ought to be said: there is an opposition between them. Catharism condemns matter, and this condemnation extends to every sort of profane love. Hence marriage was regarded as a sin: to engender flesh-and-blood offspring was to propagate matter, to continue the work of Satan the demiurge. For the majority of believers marriage was tolerated as a *pis-aller*, a necessary evil. *Fin' amors* also condemns it, but for the diametrically opposite reason: marriage was a tie arranged by contract, almost always without any choice on the part of the woman, for reasons of material, political, or family interest. Therefore courtly love lauded relationships outside marriage, provided they were not inspired by mere lust and were sanctified by love. The Cathar believer condemned love, even of the purest sort, because it bound the soul to matter; by contrast the first commandment of courtesy was love for a beautiful body. What was holy for the Provençal poets was a sin for the Cathars.

The image of the ladder figures in almost all cults. It embraces two ideas: ascent and initiation. As for the first, love is an elevation, a change of state: the lovers transcend, at least for a moment, their temporal condition and are literally transported to another world. As for the second, lovers acquire knowledge of a hidden reality. It is nonintellectual knowledge: the eye that contemplates and knows is not the eye of the intellect, as in Plato, but of the heart. A note must be added, not from religious tradition or philosophy but from feudal reality: the "service" of the lover. The lover, like the vassal, serves his beloved. The service takes place in several stages: it begins with the contemplation of the body and face of the beloved and continues, according to a ritual, to an exchange of signs and poems, which lead to a series of secret meetings. Where and when does it end? If we read the texts, we see that during the first period of Provençal poetry there was no ambiguity: the consummation of love was complete carnal fulfillment. It was a chivalrous poetry, written by noblemen and addressed to ladies of their own class. But then professional poets appear. Many of them did not belong to the aristocracy and earned their living from their poems, some of them wandering from castle to castle, others enjoying the protection of a great lord or a woman of noble lineage. The poetic convention which at the beginning turned the lord into the vassal of his lady ceased to be a poetic convention and reflected a new social reality: the poets were almost always inferior in rank to the ladies for whom they composed their songs. It was only natural that the idealism of the amorous relationship should be accentuated, though still associated with the person of the lady. The person: her soul and body.

We must not forget that the ritual of courtly love was a poetic fiction, a rule of conduct, and an idealization of social reality. It is impossible to know, therefore, to what extent its precepts were obeyed. We must also take into account the fact that during the second period of courtly love, which was its zenith, the majority of the troubadours were poets by profession and their songs expressed not so much a personal, lived experience as an ethical and aesthetic doctrine. By composing their love songs they performed a social function. But it is likewise evident that the feelings and ideas that appear in their poems corresponded more or less to what the lords, the ladies, and the clergy of the feudal courts thought, felt, and experienced in real life. With this in mind, I list the three degrees of amorous service: suitor, supplicant, and accepted lover.[7] The lady, on accepting the lover, kissed him and thereby ended his service. But there was a fourth degree: carnal lover (*drutz*). Many troubadours did not intend the relationship to lead to the *fach* (literally, the fact: copulation). This scruple was doubtless owing to the change in rank of the troubadours, who were now professional poets. Their poems did not reflect their true feelings, and furthermore the distance that separated them from their ladies was now too great. Sometimes the distance was not only by rank but age as well: the troubadour or the lady might not be young. Moreover, it was thought that physical possession killed desire and love. But Martín de Riquier points out that modern criticism "has made it clear that *fin' amors* can aspire to physical union. . . ." If such an aspiration did not exist, the genre called *alba*, which presupposes that the union between the lovers has already been consummated, would not make the slightest sense. Incidentally, these songs, as fresh as early morn, enhanced European lyric poetry from Shakespeare's nightingales to Lope de Vega's skylarks:

> Pair of nightingales
> that sings the whole night long,
> and I with my beautiful friend
> beneath the arbor in flower
> until the lookout shouts
> at the top of the tower:
> on your feet, lovers, it's time now,
> dawn is descending from the mountaintop![8]

The idea that love is an initiation implies that it is also a trial. Before physical consummation there was an intermediate step called *assag* or *assai*: a test of love. Many poems refer to this custom, among them one by the Countess of Die and another by a less-well-known *trobairitz*, Azalais de Porcairagues. The latter expressly refers to the *assai*: "Beautiful friend . . . Soon we shall reach the test [*tost en venrem a l'assai*] and I shall give myself to Your Grace." The *assai* had several degrees: attending the lady's arising in the morning or her retiring at night; contemplating her naked (the body of the woman was a microcosm, and in her contours the whole of nature, with its valleys, hills, and forests, became visible); finally, getting into her bed with her and engaging in various caresses, but without consummation (coitus interruptus).[9]

The poem "Razón de amor," which refers expressly to courtly love in its first verses, offers a charming description of the *assai*: a delightfully artificial garden—the *lugar ameno*. A balmy spring, the trees in flower, the birds, roses, lilies, sage, violets, aromatic herbs. A young man appears: he is a "scholar," he comes from France or Italy, is searching for someone, and stretches out beside a fountain. Since it is warm, he casts off his garments and drinks the cold water of the spring. A damsel of rare beauty enters the scene, and her physical features and attire are described with delight: the cape and silken petticoat, the hat, the gloves. She draws closer, cutting flowers and singing a song of love. He rises to his feet and goes to meet her; he asks her if she "knows of love"; she answers yes but that she has not yet met her friend. Finally they recognize each other by the love tokens that they have sent each other: she is the one for whom he is waiting, and he is the one she seeks. Both are devotees of courtesy. They embrace and lie down "sol olivar" (beneath the olive tree). She removes her cape and kisses him on the eyes and mouth—"tan gran sabor de mí había / sol fablar non me podía" (She so relished their flavor / she could not even speak to me). And thus, caressing each other, they while away the time together—"Un grant pieza allí estando / de nuestro amor ementando" (We tarried there / speaking of our love) until she must bid him farewell. She departs with great sorrow and vows of love. The youth remains alone and says: "Deque la ví fuera del huerto / por poco non fui muerto" (Once I saw her outside the garden / I came close to dying).

The text that has come down to us is apparently not complete; perhaps it is a fragment of a longer poem. Certain elements suggest that it is an allegory. Amid the branches of an apple tree the young man discovers two vessels. One is made of silver and contains a clear bright-red wine, left by the mistress of the garden for her friend. Is she the same maiden who takes her pleasure *sol olivar*, or is she another, who is mentioned by the damsel and who also loves him? The second vessel contains cold water. The young man says that he would gladly drink it were he not afraid that a spell has been cast on it. I will not attempt to decipher this mysterious poem; I cite it only to show, through the example of a work in Spanish, the rite of the *assai*, the love-trial.

Between courtly love and Catharism there are, to be sure, points of contact, but there are also features shared with Christianity and the Platonic tradition. These similarities are natural; what is surprising and significant is that courtly love, from the beginning, manifested itself independently and with characteristics that cannot be confused with the beliefs of the Cathars or the dogmas of the Catholic Church. It was a heresy not only for Christianity but also for Catharism and the Platonic philosophy of love—or, rather, it was a dissident view, a transgression, because essentially it was secular, experienced and felt by the laity. I have called it a cult because it had rites and faithful believers, but it was a cult in opposition to or outside churches and religions. And this is one of the traits that separate eroticism from love. Eroticism can be religious, as is the case of Tantrism and certain Gnostic sects, but love is always human. The exaltation of love was therefore not compatible with the rigorous dualism of the Cathars, nor could it be. To be sure, at the moment of the fall of Catharism, which dragged the civilization of Provence down with it, when the country was invaded by the troops of Simon de Montfort and consciences were violated by the Inquisitors, it is understandable that the Provençal poets, like the rest of the populace, showed sympathy for the Cathar cause. The French king, Louis VIII—on the pretext of extirpating a heresy, and conspiring with Pope Innocent II, who proclaimed the crusade against the Albigensians—extended the territory of his rule in the south and annihilated Occitania. In those terrible days all Occitans—Catholics and Cathars, nobles and bourgeois, common people and poets—were victims of the troops of Simon de Montfort and the cruel Dominican Inquisitors. But it is likely that if by a miracle the Cathars had triumphed, they too would have condemned courtly love.

THE REASONS THE Church of Rome had for condemning *fin' amors* were different from those of the Cathars but no less powerful. First and foremost, the attitude toward marriage. To the Church, marriage is one of the seven sacraments instituted by Jesus Christ. To attack its integrity or place its sanctity in doubt was not simply a grievous sin; it was a heresy. For the adepts of courtly love, marriage was an unjust yoke that enslaved women, whereas love outside marriage was sacred and conferred spiritual dignity on the lovers. Like the Church, they condemned adultery committed out of lust, but adultery became a sacrament if the mysterious oil of *fin' amors* anointed it. Nor could the Church approve of the rites of amorous courtesy; if the first steps, although sinful, were innocuous enough, the same could not be said for the later, extremely sensual ceremonies that constituted the *assai*. The Church condemned carnal union, even within marriage, if it did not have procreation as its purpose. Not only was courtly love indifferent to this purpose, but its rites extolled a physical pleasure diverted from reproduction.

The Church elevated chastity to the rank of the highest virtues. Its reward was ultramundane: divine grace and, for the most virtuous, the beatitude of heaven. The Provençal poets spoke endlessly in praise of a mysterious exaltation at once physical and spiritual; they called it *joi*, and it was the highest recompense of love. This *joi* was not mere happiness or sensual pleasure but an indefinable state of bliss. The terms in which certain poets describe *joi* suggest that they are referring to the pleasure of carnal climax, though refined by long expectation and *mezura*: courtly love was an aesthetic of the senses. Other poets speak of the union with nature through the contemplation of the naked beloved, which is like the sensation that stops us short when we behold a landscape or a spring morning. For still others it was an elevation of the soul similar to the transports of the mystics or the ecstasies of philosophers and contemplative poets. Happiness is by its nature inexpressible; the *joi* of the Provençals was an unusual sort of happiness and so doubly inexpressible. Only poetry could allude to this sentiment. Another difference: *joi* was not a post-mortem reward such as that bestowed upon abstinence, but a natural grace granted to lovers who had purified their desire.

But the greatest difference: the elevation of woman, who from a subject became a sovereign. Courtly love conferred upon women the most highly prized domin-ion: that of their own bodies and souls. The raising of woman was a revolution not only in the realm of the ideal but also in social reality. It is clear that courtly love did not confer political rights on women, that it was not a judicial reform: it was a change in the vision of the world. The traditional hierarchical order was up-set, and woman's social inferiority was counterbalanced by her superiority in the realm of love. In this sense it was a step toward the equality of the sexes. But in the eyes of the Church the ascent of woman was a deifi-cation. A mortal sin, to love a human being with the love we should have only for the Creator. Idolatry, a sacrilegious confusion of earthly and divine, temporal and eternal. I understand why Rougement saw in love a heresy; I also understand why W. H. Auden said that love was "a sickness of Christianity." For both there was not, nor could there be, salvation outside the Church. But understanding an idea is not the same as sharing it; I believe precisely the opposite.

In the first place, love appears in other civilizations. Is love also a heresy for Buddhism, Taoism, Vishnuism, Islam? As for love in the Western world, what theologians and their modern successors call the deification of woman was in reality a *recognition*. Each person is unique, and therefore it is not an abuse of language to speak of "the sanctity of the person." The expression, moreover, is of Christian origin. Yes, each human being, not excluding the basest of them, is the embodiment of a mystery that it is no exaggeration to call sacred. For Christians and Muslims the great mystery is the fall: of humankind, but also of the angels. The great fall of the most beautiful angel, the lieutenant of the heavenly hosts: Lucifer. Lucifer's fall prefigures and encompasses humanity's. But Lucifer, as far as we know, is irredeemable; he is doomed for all eternity. Human beings, on the other hand, can pay for their sins, can change the fall into flight. Love is the recognition, in the beloved person, of that gift of flight that characterizes all human creatures. The mystery of the human condition lies in its freedom: it is both fall and flight. And therein resides the immense allure that love has for us. It does not offer us a way of salvation; neither is it idolatry. It begins with the admiration of a person who is physically present, is followed by excitement, and culminates in the passion that leads us to happiness or disaster. Love is a test that ennobles all of us, those who are happy and those who are wretched.

THE END OF courtly love coincides with the end of the civilization of Provence. The last poets scattered; some sought refuge in Catalonia and Spain, others in Sicily and northern Italy. But before dying out, Provençal poetry enriched the rest of Europe. Through its influence the Celtic legends of the Arthurian cycle were transformed, and thanks to their popularity, courtesy became an ideal of life. Chrétien de Troyes was the first to introduce the new sensibility into the traditional subject matter of the epic. His narrative poem relating the illicit love of Lancelot and Queen Guinevere was widely imitated. But the account of Tristan and Isolde particularly stands out, the archetype of what to our own day has been called love-passion. In the story of Tristan are pagan and magic elements that give it a somber grandeur but separate it from the ideal of courtesy. For the Provençal creators of courtly love, who in this respect follow Ibn Hazm and Arabic eroticism, love is the fruit of a refined society; also, it is not a tragic passion despite the sufferings and sorrows of the lovers, because its ultimate end is *joi*, the happiness that results from the union of pleasure and contemplation, the natural and the spiritual. In the love of Tristan and Isolde the magic elements—the philter that the lovers drink by mistake—emphasize the irrational power of eroticism. The only escape for the victims of that power is death. The opposition between this dark vision of passion and the idea of courtesy, which sees passion as a purifying process that leads to illumination, is the essence of the mystery of love. A twofold fascination in the face of life and death, love is fall and flight, choice and submission.

The influence of the literature that commingled pagan legend with courtesy was immense. A celebrated episode of the *Divina Commedia* illustrates the power that this exercised over people's minds. In the second circle of hell, that of the lustful, Dante meets Paolo and Francesca. When questioned by the poet, Francesca tells him how, one day, as she and Paolo were reading together a book recounting the story of the love of Lancelot and Guinevere, they discovered the love that they felt for each other and that led to their death. On reaching the passage in which Lancelot and Guinevere, united by their passion, kiss each other for the first time, they stopped reading, looked at each other, blushed and paled. Then

> questi, che mai da me non fia diviso,
> la bocca me basciò tutto tremante.
>
> (He who is one with me, alive and dead
> Breathed on my lips the tremor of his kiss.)[10]

And Francesca comments: "Quel giorno non vi leggemmo avante" (That day we read no further). There has been much discussion as to whether Dante took pity on the ill-starred couple. What is certain is that, on hearing their story and seeing them in hell, he fainted.

Following approved theology, the fate of the sinners can only arouse disgust or repulsion in us. The contrary would be blasphemy: questioning God's justice. But Dante too was a sinner, and his sins were above all sins of love, as Beatrice reminds him more than once. Perhaps for that reason and because of the sympathy he felt toward Francesca—he was a friend of her family —he changed the story slightly: for in the romance it is Guinevere who kisses Lancelot first.

Dante intended to reconcile within himself the

theologian and the poet, but he never completely succeeded. Like all the practitioners of the *dolce stil nuovo*,
he knew and admired the Provençal poets. In the episode with Paolo and Francesca he refers twice to the
doctrine of courtly love. The first reference is an echo
of his master, Guido Guinicelli, who viewed love as an
aristocracy of the heart: "Amor, ch' al cor gentil ratto
s' aprende" (Love, which is quickly kindled in the gentle heart). Love is a spiritual brotherhood, and only
those with a gentle nature are really capable of loving.
The second reference repeats one of the maxims of André le Chapelain: "Amor, ch'a nullo amato amar per-
dona" (Love, which absolves no beloved one from
loving). Love commands, and for the noble soul dis-
obeying it is impossible. By repeating this maxim, does
Francesca not absolve herself for her sinful love? But
is this absolution not another sin? What did Dante really think of all this?

He radically changed courtly love when he incor-
porated it into Scholastic theology, thereby reducing the
opposition between love and Christianity. By introduc-
ing a feminine figure of salvation, Beatrice, as the intermediary between heaven and earth, he changed the
nature of the relationship between lover and lady. Beatrice continued to occupy a lofty position, but the bond

between her and Dante was altered. There are those who have pondered the question: Was it really love? But if it was not, why did she intercede for one sinner in particular? Love is exclusive; charity is not. To prefer one person to others is a sin against charity. Thus, Dante is still caught in the trap of courtly love. Beatrice, in the sphere of love, fulfills a function analogous to that of the Virgin Mary, except that she is not a universal intercessor: she is moved by love for one person. There is ambiguity in the figure of Beatrice: she is love, and she is charity. I will add another ambiguity: she is married. Here too Dante follows courtly love, and in one of its most daring transgressions of Christian morality. How to justify the solicitude with which Beatrice watches over Dante's spiritual salvation if it is not through the intervention of love?

Laura, Petrarch's beloved, was also a married woman (and incidentally an ancestor of the Marquis de Sade). This is no coincidence: both poets were faithful to the rule of courtly love. The fact is particularly significant in that Dante and Petrarch were very different poets, and their concepts of love were different. Petrarch has a less powerful mind than Dante; his poetry does not embrace the totality of human destiny, suspended by the thread of time between two eternities. But his idea of love is more modern: the beloved is not a messenger from heaven, nor does she afford the poet a glimpse of supernatural mysteries. Her love is ideal, not heavenly; Laura is a lady, not a saint. Petrarch's poems do not tell of visions; they are subtle analyses of feeling. The poet is fond of antitheses—fire and ice, light and darkness, flight and fall, pleasure and pain—because he himself is the theater of a battle between opposing passions.

Dante the straight line; Petrarch the continual zigzag. The latter's contradictions paralyze him until a new contradiction sets him in motion once again. Each sonnet is an ethereal architecture that fades away, to be reborn in another sonnet. The *Canzionere*, unlike the *Commedia*, is not the account of a pilgrimage and an ascent; Petrarch experiences and describes an endless debate with himself and within himself. His life is directed inward, and he speaks only with his inner *I*. He is the first modern poet, by which I mean the first to be aware of his contradictions and the first to transform them into the substance of poetry. Almost all European love poetry can be looked upon as a series of glosses, variations, and transgressions of the *Canzionere*. Many poets are superior to Petrarch in one way or another, but very seldom are they superior overall. I am thinking of Ronsard, Donne, Quevedo, Lope de Vega, in short, of the great lyric poets of the Renaissance and Baroque. At the end of his life Petrarch suffered a spiritual crisis and renounced love: he regarded it as an aberration that had endangered his salvation, as he tells us in *Secretum*, his confessions. His master here was St. Augustine, another man of intense passions and more sensual than he. Petrarch's retraction was also a homage: a recognition of the power of love.

The Provençal legacy to love poetry was twofold: forms and ideas. It has been passed on to us through Dante, Petrarch, and their successors, down to the Surrealist poets of the twentieth century. It is alive not only in the highest forms of the art and literature of the West but also in songs, films, and popular myths. In the beginning the transmission was direct: Dante spoke the Limousin dialect, and in *Purgatory*, when Arnaut Daniel appears, he has him speak in verse and in the *langue d'oc*. Cavalcanti, who traveled throughout the south of France, also knew Provençal. The same is true of all the poets of that generation. Although today only a handful of people speak the *langue d'oc*, the tradition of Provençal poetry has not disappeared. The history of courtly love, its changes and metamorphoses, is not just that of our art and literature: it is the history of our sensibility and of the myths that have set many imaginations on fire from the twelfth century to our own day. The history of Western civilization.

1. All the texts I mention immediately below have appeared in various volumes of the Spanish edition of my complete works (*Obras Completas*): "Apariencia desnuda" (The Works of Marcel Duchamp), in *Los Privilegios de la vista*, I, vol. 6, 223–247; "Concilio de Luceros," in *Sor Juana de la Cruz o Las trampas de la fe*, vol. 5; and "Quevedo, Heráclito y algunos sonetos," in *Fundación y disidencia*, vol. 3, 125–137.

2. The abbey of Fontevrault, run by an abbess whom Guillermo called "the abbess of whores."

3. René Nelli, *L'Erotique des troubadours*, Toulouse, 1963.

4. According to García Gómez, *The Book of the Flower* probably dates from 890 and *The Necklace of the Dove* from 1022. In his extensive introduction to the latter (Madrid: Alianza Editorial, 1971), García Gómez makes an interesting comparison between the ideas of Ibn Hazm and those of the Archpriest of Hita. We stand in need of a good modern essay on the Archpriest's *El libro de buen amor*.

5. *The Art of Courtly Love*, edited and translated by J. J. Parry, with an introduction, New York, 1941.

6. Cathar is from the Greek *kátharos*: pure.

7. René Nelli, *L'Erotique des troubadours*.

8. Anonymous. Free version by Octavio Paz, translation by Helen Lane.

9. I have commented on this ceremony in the final pages of "Apariencia desnuda," *Obras Completas*, vol. 6.

10. From John Ciardi's translation of *The Inferno* (New York: New American Library, 1954), 62.

A Solar System

I f w e r e v i e w Western literature of the eight centuries that separate us from courtly love, we notice immediately that an immense number of the poems, works
for the theater, and novels have love as their subject.
One of the functions of literature is the representation
of the passions, and the preponderance of the amatory
theme shows that love has been a principal passion of
the men and women of the West. Another has been
power, from political ambition to the hunger for material goods or honors. In the course of these eight centuries, has what the Provençal poets bequeathed us

changed? Answering this question requires more than a moment's reflection. There have been so many changes that it is almost impossible to enumerate them, and it would be no less difficult to attempt an analysis of every variation of the amatory passion. From the lady of the Provençal poets to Anna Karenina a great deal of water has flowed under the bridge. The changes began with Dante and have continued to our day. Each poet and novelist has his or her own vision of love, and some have a number of visions embodied in different characters. Perhaps the writer richest in characters is Shakespeare: Juliet, Ophelia, Mark Antony, Rosalind, Othello. . . . Each is love personified, and each is unlike the others. As much can be said of Balzac and his gallery of men and women in love, from an aristocrat like the Duchess of Langeais to a plebeian out of a brothel like Esther Gobseck, Balzac's characters come from all classes and the four cardinal points of the compass. He even dared break with a convention that had been respected since the era of courtly love, for it is in his oeuvre that homosexual love appears for the first time: the chaste and sublimated passion of the former convict Vautrin for Lucien de Rubempré, a "skirt chaser," and the love of the Marquise of San Real for Paquita Valdès, the *fille aux yeux d'or*. Confronted with such variety, we might well conclude that the history of European and American literatures is the history of the metamorphoses of love.

The moment I have set it down, I feel the need to amend and tone down my conclusion: for none of these changes has essentially altered the archetype created in the twelfth century. There are certain distinctive aspects of courtly love—no more than five, as will be seen—that are present in all the love stories of our literature, and that furthermore have been the basis of our ideas and images of this sentiment since the Middle Ages. Some conventions have disappeared, such as the lady's being a married woman of the nobility, or the lovers belonging to different sexes. The rest remains—that totality of antithetical conditions that distinguish love from the other passions: attraction/election, freedom/submission, fidelity/betrayal, soul/body. Truly astonishing is the continuity of our idea of love, not its changes and variations. Francesca is a victim of love, the Marquise de Merteuil is a victimizer, and Fabricio del Dongo triumphantly eludes the trap that seals Romeo's doom, but the passion that exalts them or devours them is the same. All are heroes and heroines of love, that peculiar sentiment that is simultaneously a fatal compulsion and a free choice.

One of the defining attributes of modern literature is criticism; what I mean to say is that, unlike the literatures of the past, modern literature not only sings of heroes and their rise and fall but also analyzes them. Don Quixote is not Achilles, and on his deathbed he devotes himself to a bitter examination of his conscience. Rastignac is not pious Aeneas; he knows that he is merciless, feels no remorse for this, and cynically confesses it to himself. An intense poem by Baudelaire is titled "L'examen de minuit." The favorite object of all this examination and analysis is amorous passion. Modern poetry, novels, and works for the theater are remarkable for the number, profundity, and subtlety of their studies of love, to the accompaniment of obsessions, emotions, sensations. Many of these studies— Stendhal's, for example—have been dissections. The surprising thing, however, is that in each case the mental surgery ends in a resurrection. In the final pages of *L'education sentimentale*, perhaps Flaubert's most perfect work, the hero and a friend of his youth sum up their lives: "One of us dreamed of love, the other of power, and we both failed. Why?" Frédéric Moreau, the main character, answers: "Perhaps the failure lay in the straight line." In other words, passion is inflexible and knows nothing of compromise. A revealing answer, especially when the reader notes that the one who speaks these words is an alter ego of Flaubert. But Frédéric-Flaubert is not disappointed in love; despite his failure, it still seems for him that love was the best thing that happened to him, the one thing that justified his life. Flaubert does not belittle love; without illusions he describes bourgeois society, that detestable fabric of compromises, weaknesses, perfidies, betrayals great and small, ignominious selfishness. He was not naive but wise when he said: *"Madame Bovary, c'est moi."* Emma Bovary, like himself, was not a victim of love but of her society and class. What would have become of her had she not lived in a sordid French province? Dante condemns the world from the perspective of heaven; modern literature condemns it from the perspective of outraged personal awareness.

The continuity of our idea of love still awaits an account of its history; the variety of forms it assumes awaits an encyclopedia. But there is another method closer to geography than to history and cataloging: a sketch of the boundaries between love and the other passions, a sketch of the kind that traces the outline of an island in an archipelago. And this is what I am attempting to do in these reflections.

LET US BEGIN with the boundaries of sexuality, eroticism, and love. The three are modes, manifestations of life. Biologists are still debating the question of what life is. For some it is a word that has no meaning; what we call life is merely a chemical phenomenon, the result of the combination of a number of acids. I confess that such simplifications have never convinced me. Even if life began on our planet through the association of a few acids, it is impossible to reduce to chemical reactions the evolution of living matter from protozoans to mammals. What is true is that the transition from sexuality to love is characterized not so much by a growing complexity as by the intervention of an agent that bears the name of a beautiful Greek princess: Psyche. Sexuality is animal; eroticism is human. It is a phenomenon that manifests itself within a society and that essentially consists of turning aside or changing the reproductive sexual impulse into a representation. Love is also ceremony and representation, but it is something else besides: a purification, as the Provençal poets said, that transforms the subject and object of the erotic encounter into unique persons. Love is the final metaphor of sexuality. Its cornerstone is freedom: the mystery of the person.

There is no love without eroticism, just as there can be no eroticism without sexuality. True, it is sometimes difficult to distinguish between love and eroticism: in the violently sensual passion that united Paolo and Francesca, for example. But the fact that they suffered their punishment together, without ever wanting to be separated, reveals that what united them was really love. Their adultery was a serious matter—Paolo was the brother of Giovanni Malatesta, Francesca's husband—but love refined their lust. Passion, which keeps them united in hell, ennobles them even if it does not grant them salvation.

It is easier to distinguish between love and emotions less saturated with sexuality. We are said to love our country, our religion, our party, certain principles and ideas. But it is clear that in none of these cases is it a question of what we call love—in all of them the erotic element is missing, the attraction to a body. One loves a person, not an abstraction. The word love is also used to designate the affection we feel for people with whom we have blood ties: parents, children, brothers and sisters, and other relatives. In these relationships none of the elements of the amorous passion appears: the discovery of the beloved person, generally someone we do not know; physical and spiritual attraction; the obstacle that separates the lovers; the search for reciprocity; and, finally, the act of choosing a single person from among all the others who surround us. We love our parents and our children because religion, custom, the moral law, or the law of kinship so decrees. I will be asked: And is the Oedipus or Electra complex, the attraction toward a father or mother, not erotic? This question deserves an answer apart.

The famous complex, whatever its real biological and psychological truth may be, is closer to sexuality than to eroticism. According to Freud, the entire unconscious process beneath the tyranny of the superego consists precisely in the displacement of this first sexual appetite, in the directing of it toward a different object, a substitute for the image of the father or mother. If the Oedipal tendency is not thus redirected, neurosis—and in some cases incest—takes place. If incest takes place without the consent of one of the participants, it is rape, violation, deception, whatever one chooses to call it, but it is not love. It is another matter if there is a mutual attraction and a free acceptance of that attraction—but then family affection disappears: it is no longer a question of parents and children but of lovers. But incest between parents and children is infrequent. The probable reason is the difference in age: by the time of puberty, the father and mother have ceased to be objects of desire. Among animals the incest taboo does not exist, but in them the transition from being young to being sexually mature is extremely brief. Human incest is almost never voluntary. Lot's two daughters got their father drunk two nights in a row in order to lie with him, first one, then the other. As for paternal incest, every day we read stories in the press of fathers who sexually abuse their sons or daughters. None of this bears any relationship to what we call love.

For Freud the passions are mirrors; we believe we love X, his or her body and soul, but in reality we love in X the image of Y. A spectral sexuality that turns everything it touches into reflections. In literature, incest between parents and offspring does not take place as a freely accepted passion: Oedipus *does not know* that he is Jocasta's son. The exceptions are Sade and a few others; their subject is not love but eroticism and its perversions. On the other hand, love between siblings is featured in a splendid work by John Ford, *'Tis Pity She's a Whore*, and in memorable pages of Robert Musil's novel *The Man without Qualities*. In these examples—there are others—blind attraction, once it is recognized, is accepted and chosen. But this is the complete opposite of family affection, where the voluntary element, choice, does not appear. None of us chooses our parents, our children, our brothers and sisters; but we all choose our lovers, male and female.

Filial, fraternal, paternal and maternal love are not love: they are *piety*, in the oldest and most religious sense of the word. *Piety* comes from the Latin *pietas*. It is the name of the virtue, the *Diccionario de Autoridades* tells us, that "moves and incites to revere, respect, serve, and honor God, our parents, and our country." *Pietas* is the devotion professed for the gods in Rome. *Pietas* also means *pity*, and for Christians it is an aspect of charity. French and English, distinguishing between the two meanings, have two words to express it: *piété* and *piety* respectively for the first, and for the second, *pitié* and *pity*. Piety or love of God springs, according to the theologians, from the feeling of abandonment: human beings, God's children, feel that they have been flung headlong into the world and so seek their Creator. It is a fundamental experience, literally, because it is intimately associated with our birth. A great deal has been written about the subject. I confine myself here to emphasizing that it consists of the knowledge that we have been expelled from the prenatal whole and thrust into an alien world: this life. Thus the love of God, that is to say, of the Father and Creator, bears a strong resemblance to filial piety. I have already pointed out that the affection we feel for our parents is involuntary. Nor is love for our fellow humans love: it is charity. A pretty countess of Balzac's summed up all of the foregoing with admirable, concise impertinence, in a letter to a suitor: "Je puis faire, je vous l'avoue, une infinité de choses par charité, tout, excepté l'amour" (I can do, I assure you, no end of things out of charity, everything but make love.)[1]

The mystic experience goes beyond piety. Mystic poets have compared their trials and ecstasies to love. They have done so with accents of touching sincerity and passionately sensual images. Erotic poets, for their part, use religious terms to express their transports. Our mystic poetry is suffused with eroticism and our amorous poetry with religiosity. In this respect we depart from the Greco-Roman tradition and resemble the Muslims and Hindus. A number of attempts have been made to explain this strange affinity between mysticism and eroticism, but in my opinion none have succeeded. I add, in passing, an observation that might help shed a little more light on the phenomenon. The act in which the erotic experience culminates, orgasm, is inexpressible. It is a sensation that goes from extreme tension to the most complete self-surrender and from single-minded concentration to the forgetfulness of self. The reuniting of opposites, in the space of a second: the affirmation of the ego and its dissolution, ascent and fall, there and here, time and timelessness. The mystic experience is likewise inexpressible: instantaneous fusion of opposites, tension and release of tension, affirmation and negation, being outside oneself and rejoining oneself in the heart of a reconciled nature.

It is only natural that the mystic and erotic poets should use similar language: there are not many ways to express the inexpressible. But their difference leaps to the eye: in love the object is a mortal being, while in the mystical experience it is a timeless being who momentarily assumes a form. Romeo weeps on seeing Juliet's dead body; the mystic sees resurrection in Christ's wounds. The obverse and reverse sides of the same phenomenon: the lover sees and touches a presence; the mystic contemplates an apparition. In the mystic vision a human being engages in a dialogue with his Creator, or, in the case of the Buddhist mystic, with Emptiness, and the dialogue begins—if it is possible to speak of a dialogue—between discontinuous human time and the seamless time of eternity, a present that never changes, never increases or decreases but remains ever identical to itself. Human love is the union of two beings subject to time and its accidents: change, sickness, death. Although it does not save us from time, it opens it a crack, so that in a flash love's contradictory nature is manifest:

that vivacity which endlessly destroys itself and is reborn, which is always both now and never. Therefore
all love, even the most blissful, is tragic.

FRIENDSHIP IS OFTEN compared to love. Sometimes as complementary passions, sometimes, more frequently, as opposites. If the carnal, physical element is
omitted, the resemblance between love and friendship
is obvious. Both are freely chosen affections, imposed
neither by law nor by custom, and both are interpersonal. We are friends of a person, not of a multitude;
unless the phrase is used derisively, nobody can be
called "a friend of the human race." Choice and exclusivity are conditions that friendship shares with love.
But we can be in love with a person who does not love
us, whereas friendship is impossible if it is not recip-
rocated. Another difference: friendship does not come
about at first sight; it is a more complex sentiment. The
affinity of ideas, feelings, inclinations. At the beginning
of love there is surprise, the discovery of *another person*
to whom we are bound by no tie other than an indefinable physical and spiritual attraction; that person may
even be a stranger and come from another world.
Friendship is born of community and concordance.
Congeniality is the result; having dealings with a person

refines and transforms congeniality into friendship. Love is born of a sudden infatuation; friendship from frequent contact and prolonged interaction. Love is instantaneous; friendship takes time.

To the ancients, friendship was superior to love. According to Aristotle, friendship is "a virtue or is accompanied by virtue; furthermore, it is the most necessary thing in life."[2] Plutarch, Cicero, and others followed his example in their praise of friendship. In other civilizations it has enjoyed equal prestige. Among the great legacies of China to the world is its poetry, and in it the theme of friendship is preponderant, along with the feeling for nature and the solitude of the sage. Meetings, farewells, and evocations of a distant friend are frequent in Chinese poetry, as in this poem by Wang Wei on bidding a friend farewell at the frontiers of the Empire:

FAREWELL TO YÜAN, SENT TO ANSI

In Wei. A light rain wets the fine dust.
In the inn green willows greener still.
"Listen, friend, let us have another drink together.
Once beyond the Yang Pass there is no 'listen, friend.' "[3]

Aristotle says that there are three kinds of friendship: friendship out of interest or usefulness, friendship out of pleasure, and "perfect friendship, that of good men of similar virtue, because each equally desires the good for the other." To desire the good for the other is to desire it for oneself, if the friend is a good man. The first two kinds of friendship are circumstantial and destined to last only a short time: the third is enduring and one of the highest goods to which man can aspire. I say man in the literal and restricted sense of the word: Aristotle is not referring to women. His classification is an ethical one and may not correspond altogether to reality: is a bad man unable to be the friend of a good man? Pylades, a model of friendship, does not hesitate to aid his friend Orestes in the murder of the latter's mother, Clytemnestra, and of Aegisthus, her lover.

Pondering the reason for the friendship that united him to the poet Étienne de La Boétie, Montaigne answers his own question: "Because he was he and I was I." And he adds that in all this "there was an inexplicable and foreordained force, the intermediary of this union." A lover would not have answered differently. However, it is impossible to confuse love with friendship, and in the same essay Montaigne takes it upon himself to distinguish them: "Although love too is born of choice, it occupies a different place from that of friendship. . . . Its fire, I confess, is more active, penetrating, and harsh. But it is a rash and changeable fire . . . a feverish fire," whereas "friendship is an even and universal heat, temperate, moreover, and moderate . . . a constant and calm heat, all gentleness and polish, without asperities."[4] Friendship is an eminently social virtue and more enduring than love. For young people, Aristotle says, it is easy to acquire friends, but they can be forsaken with equal ease: friendship is an affection more characteristic of maturity. I am not entirely convinced of this, but I do believe that friendship is less subject to unexpected change than love. Almost always, love manifests itself as a rupture or violation of the social order; it is a challenge to the customs and institutions of the community. A passion that, uniting the lovers, separates them from society. A republic of lovers would be ungovernable; the political ideal of a civilized society—which has never been realized—would be a republic of friends.

Is the distance between love and friendship unbridgeable? Is it impossible for us to be friends with our lovers? Montaigne's opinion—and here he follows the ancients—is decidedly negative. Marriage strikes him as being unfavorable to friendship: an obligatory union intended to last a lifetime, even though it was chosen freely, marriage is the theater of so many and such diverse interests and passions that there is no room left in it for friendship. I disagree. For one thing, modern marriage is no longer indissoluble, nor does it have a great deal to do with marriage as Montaigne knew it. For another thing, friendship between husband and wife—a fact we note every day—is one of the features that redeem the marriage bond. Montaigne's negative opinion extends, moreover, to love itself. He grants that it would be most desirable if the very souls and bodies of lovers enjoyed the union provided by friendship, but the soul of woman does not seem to him to be "strong enough to endure the constraints of such a tight and long-lasting bond." Therefore he agrees with the ancients: the female sex is incapable of friendship.

It is true that neither in history nor in literature are there many examples of friendship between women. This is not altogether surprising: for century after century—since the Neolithic, according to some anthropologists—women have lived in obscurity. What do we know of what the wives of Athens, the girls of Jerusalem, the peasant women of the twelfth century, or the bourgeoises of the fifteenth felt and thought? Whenever we learn a little more about a given historical period, outstanding women, who were the friends of philosophers, poets, and artists, turn up: St. Paula, Vittoria Colonna, Madame de Sévigné, George Sand, Virginia Woolf, Hannah Arendt, and so many others. Exceptions? Yes, but friendship, like love, is always exceptional. This having been said, I grant that all the cases I have cited involve friendships between men and women. Thus far friendship between women is much rarer than friendship between men. In relationships between women, backbiting, envy, gossip, jealousy, and petty perfidies are frequent. Which is almost certainly owing not to any innate inability of women but to their social situation. Perhaps their progressive liberation will change all this. Let us hope so. Friendship requires esteem, with the result that the value of a woman is reappraised. . . . I return to Montaigne: it seems to me that he was not entirely wrong to regard love and friendship as incompatible. They are different affections or, as he puts it, different fires. But he was wrong when he declared that women are incapable of friendship. Nor is the opposition between love and friendship absolute: not only do the two share many qualities, but love can turn into friendship. It is, I would say, one of its denouements, as we see in certain marriages. Love and friendship are rare, extremely rare, passions. We must not confuse them either with passing affairs or with what people very often call "intimate" relationships. I said earlier that love is tragic; I add here that friendship is a response to tragedy.

ONCE THE BOUNDARIES—sometimes fluctuating, imprecise—between love and the other affections have been traced, we can take another look at those affections and determine their basic elements. I say basic because they have been the same since the beginning: they have survived eight centuries of history. At the same time, the relationships between them change continually and produce new combinations, like the particles of modern physics. The variety of the forms of amorous passion is owed to this constant interaction of influences. I would call them a cluster of relations, like the one imagined by Roman Jakobson on the most basic level of language, the phonological, between sound and sense, whose combinations and permutations produce meaning. It is not surprising, therefore, that many people have been tempted to outline a system of the erotic passions. An undertaking that no one has been able to carry out successfully. Personally I believe it is impossible: we should not forget that love is, as Dante said, an accident—a contingency—in the life of a human being, and that that being is unpredictable. It is more useful to isolate the elements or distinctive features of this affect we call love. I emphasize that it is not a question of a definition or of a catalog, but of a reconnaissance—in the primary meaning of the word: a careful examination to recognize a thing's particular nature. I will use some of the conclusions already reached here, but in conjunction with other observations, other conjectures: a recapitulation, a critique, and a hypothesis.

When I attempted to organize my ideas in an orderly fashion, I found that even though certain characteristics of our image of love have disappeared and others changed, some have resisted the erosion and mutations of the centuries. They can be reduced to five and make up what I have made so bold as to call the basic elements. The first element of love is exclusivity. In these pages I have referred to it several times, arguing that it marks the boundary between love and the larger territory of eroticism. Eroticism is social and appears in all places and eras. There is no society without erotic rites and practices, from the most innocuous to the most bloody. Eroticism is the human dimension of sexuality, what imagination adds to nature. An example: copulation face to face, in which the two participants look into each other's eyes, is a human invention and not a practice of any of the other mammals. But love is individual, or, more exactly, interpersonal: we want only one person, and we ask that person to love us with the same exclusivity. Exclusivity requires reciprocity, the assent of the other, his or her free will. Hence the exclusivity of love entails another of its basic elements: freedom. Yet another proof of what I pointed out earlier, that none of the basic elements has a life of its own: each is related to the others; each determines the others and is determined by them.

Yet each is invariable. The exclusivity of love is an absolute condition: without it there can be no love. But it is not the sole condition: the other elements must participate as well, to a greater or lesser degree. The desire for exclusivity alone can be mere eagerness for possession. This was the passion analyzed with such subtlety by Marcel Proust. True love consists precisely of the transformation of the appetite for possession into surrender. This is why love seeks reciprocity and hence radically departs from the old relationship of domination and servitude. The exclusivity of love is the foundation of all the other elements, the focal point around which the others revolve. The requirement of exclusivity is a mystery: Why do we love this person and not another? A mystery explained only by recourse to other mysteries, such as the myth of the androgyne in the *Symposium*. The exclusivity of love is a facet of another great mystery: the human person.

Many gradations and nuances lie between exclusivity

and promiscuity. We say that without exclusivity there can be no love, but isn't infidelity the daily bread of couples? It is indeed. Which proves that Ibn Hazm, Guinicelli, Shakespeare, and Stendhal were not wrong: that love is a passion almost everyone venerates but that few, very few, actually experience. Of course, in this as in everything else, there are degrees. Infidelity may be a matter of consent or not, and either frequent or occasional. If practiced by only one partner, it causes the other suffering and humiliation. The unfaithful party is insensitive, cruel, incapable of true love. If the infidelity is by mutual consent, engaged in by both parties, there may be a lowering of the tension of passion: the couple, lacking the strength to do what passion requires, decides to relativize the relationship. Is this love? It is, rather, erotic complicity. Many people say that in such cases passion turns into friendship. Montaigne would have immediately protested: friendship is an affection as exclusive as love, or even more so. Permission to be unfaithful is an arrangement, or a resignation. But love is strict, and like libertinism, although in the opposite direction, an asceticism. If Sade saw with extraordinary clear-sightedness that the libertine aspires to insensibility, to see the Other only as an object, the person in love seeks total union and therefore turns the object into a subject. As for occasional infidelity, it too is a failing, a weakness. It can and should be forgiven, because we are imperfect beings, and everything we do is marked by the stigma of our original imperfection. And what if we love two persons at the same time? That is always a matter of a temporary conflict: often it comes about at the moment of transition between one love and another. Choice, which is the proof of love, invariably resolves the conflict, at times cruelly. It seems to me that these examples suffice to show that exclusivity, though it is seldom adhered to wholly, is the necessary condition for love.

THE SECOND ELEMENT is polemical in nature: obstacle and transgression. It is not for nothing that love has been compared to war. Among the famous loves of Greek mythology, in which erotic scandals abound, is the affair of Venus and Mars. The dialogue between obstacle and desire appears in all love relationships and always assumes the form of a combat. From the lady of the troubadours, an incarnation of distance—geographical, social, or spiritual—love has continually been both interdiction and infraction, impediment and contravention. All couples, whether of poems and novels or the stage and screen, confront some taboo and break it, with varying results, often tragic. In the past the obstacle was mainly a social one. In the West, love began in feudal courts, in a markedly hierarchical society. The subversive power of courtly love is a double violation of the feudal code: the lady must be married, and her lover, the troubadour, must be of inferior rank. At the end of the seventeenth century, both in Spain and in the capitals of the viceroyalties of Mexico and Peru, there appears a curious erotic custom which is the symmetrical counterpart of courtly love. It was called palace courting. When the court was established in Madrid, the families of the nobility sent their daughters there as the queen's ladies-in-waiting. The young women lived in the royal palace and participated in its festivities and ceremonies. Erotic relationships formed between these ladies-in-waiting and the courtiers. The courtiers, however, were usually married, so the affairs were illicit and temporary. For the young ladies-in-waiting, palace courting was a sort of school for amatory initiation, not far removed from the courtesy of medieval love.[5]

With the passage of time the prohibitions from rank and clan rivalries lessened, though they did not completely disappear. It is unthinkable that the enmity between two families such as the Capulets and the Montagues could thwart the love of two young people in a modern city. But today there are other prohibitions no less rigid and cruel—and many of the old ones have grown stronger. The taboo based on race is still in effect, not because it is enforced by law but because of custom and prejudice. The Moor Othello would find that when it comes to sexual relations between people of different races most people in New York, London, or Paris are not less but more intolerant than those of sixteenth-century Venice. Alongside the barrier of blood stand social and economic obstacles. Although today the distance between rich and poor, the bourgeoisie and the proletariat, does not have the rigid and trenchant form that divided master from servant or courtier from commoner, obstacles based on class and money still affect sexual relations. A gap between reality and legislation: this is not to be found in legal codes but in customs. Everyday life, not to mention novels or films, abounds in love stories whose impediment is a taboo based on class or race.

Another prohibition that still has not altogether disappeared is the one regarding homosexuality, whether masculine or feminine. It was condemned by the churches and for a long time called the "abominable sin." Today our societies—I am speaking of large cities—are somewhat more tolerant than a few years ago, but the anathema persists in many milieus. Let us not forget that barely a century ago it caused Oscar Wilde's disgrace. Our literature has avoided the subject or disguised it. We all know, for example, that Albertine, Gilberte, and the other *jeunes filles en fleur* were in reality boys—Gide displayed great courage by publishing *Corydon*. E. M. Forster's novel *Maurice*, in accordance with his wishes, appeared only after his death. Certain modern poets were more daring, and among them a Spaniard stands out: Louis Cernuda. One must remember the time and the language in which Cernuda published his poems in order to appreciate their boldness.

The most rigorous and feared prohibitions of the past were those of the churches. In modern, predominantly secular societies they are less heeded. But this gain has been a relative one: the twentieth century has preserved religious hatred by converting it into ideological passion. Totalitarian states not only took the place of ecclesiastical inquisitions, but their tribunals were more pitiless and obtuse. One of the victories of modern democracy had been to deliver private life—the individual's sacred domain—from the control of the state. The totalitarians took a step backward and even dared pass laws having to do with love. The Nazis forbade Germans to have sexual relations with non-Aryans. They conceived eugenic programs to perfect and purify the "German race," as if it were a breed of horse or dog.

The Communists were no less intolerant; their obsession was not race but ideological purity. The memory of the humiliations and outrages that citizens under Communist rule had to endure in order to marry persons from the "free world" still lingers. One of the great novels of our era on the theme of love—Boris Pasternak's *Doctor Zhivago*—tells the story of two lovers separated by the hatreds of ideological factions during the civil war that followed the seizure of power by the Bolsheviks. Politics is a great enemy of love. But lovers always find a moment to escape. That moment is minute and immense: a blink of an eye that lasts a century. The Provençal poets and the Romantics of the nineteenth century would have smiled and nodded in approval at Pasternak's description of the ecstasy of the lovers isolated in a cabin on the steppe as men slit each other's throats over abstractions. The Russian poet compares their caresses and broken phrases with the dialogues on love of the ancient philosophers. He was not exaggerating: for the lovers, the body thinks and the soul can be touched.

OBSTACLE/TRANSGRESSION IS intimately associated with another element that is also double: domination/submission. The model for courtly love was the feudal relationship: the ties that united vassal and master. But putting a real relationship of domination into the sphere of love—a privileged realm of the imaginary—was more than a transposition or reproduction. The vassal was bound to his lord by an obligation that began at the moment of his birth and was symbolically manifested by the formal public rendering of his vows of homage, fealty, and service. The relationship between sovereign and subject was reciprocal and a given; that is to say, it was not by explicit agreement where free choice played a part but, rather, the result of two circumstances: birth and the soil on which one was born. The love relationship, on the other hand, is based on a fiction: the code of courtesy. By copying the relationship between feudal lord and vassal, the lover transforms the givens of blood and soil into an act of freedom: he voluntarily chooses his lady, and by this choice chooses also his servitude. The code of courtly love contains, moreover, another transgression against the aristocratic world: the noble lady voluntarily forgets her rank and parts with her sovereignty.

Love has been and is still the great act of subversion in the West. As with eroticism, the agent of the transformation is imagination. Except that in the case of love the transformation results in an opposite relationship: it does not deny the Other or reduce the Other to a shadow but is instead the negation of one's own sovereignty. This self-negation has a counterpart: the acceptance of the Other. The image, contrary to what happens in the realm of eroticism, takes on substance; the Other, male or female, is now not a shadow but a carnal and spiritual reality. I can not only touch it but *talk* to it as well. And I can hear it—and drink in its words. Transubstantiation once again: the body becomes a voice, a meaning, a soul. Every love, then, is eucharistic.

The eagerness of all those in love and the subject of our great poets and novelists has always been the same: the recognition of the beloved. Recognition in the sense of acknowledging, as the dictionary states, the subordinate position in which one finds oneself. The paradox lies in the fact that the recognition is voluntary, freely given. Recognition also in the sense of confessing that we are in the presence of a mystery in the flesh: a person. Recognition aspires to reciprocity but is independent of it. It is a wager no one is certain of winning because its outcome depends on the freedom of the Other. Vassalage is the given, reciprocal obligation of overlord and tenant; love is the search for a freely granted reciprocity. But here is another mystery: the transformation of the erotic object into a person immediately makes that person a subject who possesses free will. The object I desire becomes a subject who desires me—or rejects me. The giving up of personal sovereignty and the voluntary acceptance of servitude involves a genuine change of nature: by way of the bridge of mutual desire the object becomes desiring subject and the subject becomes desired object. Love, then, is represented in the form of a knot. A knot made of two intertwined freedoms.

DOMINATION AND SUBMISSION, like obstacle and transgression, are not elements in and of themselves but part of a vaster contradiction: fate and freedom. Love is the involuntary attraction toward a person and the voluntary acceptance of that attraction. There has been a great deal of discussion about the nature of the impulse that leads us to fall in love. For Plato attraction was a composite of two desires fused into one: the desire for beauty and the desire for immortality. We desire a beautiful body—and to engender beautiful children by way of that body. This desire, as we have seen, is gradually transformed until it culminates, purified now, in the contemplation of essences and ideas. But neither love nor eroticism, as I believe I have shown in this book, is necessarily associated with the desire for reproduction. As for beauty: for Plato it was one and eternal; for us it is plural and mutable. There are as many ideas of physical beauty as there are civilizations and eras. The beauty of today is not what inflamed the imagination of our grandparents; exoticism scarcely appreciated by Plato's contemporaries is today an erotic stimulus. In a poem by Rubén Darío that shocked and dazzled its readers a hundred years ago, the poet experiences every possible erotic encounter with Spanish, German, Chinese, French, Ethiopian, and Italian women. Love, he says, is a cosmopolitan passion.

BUT BEAUTY PLAYS only a minor role in amorous attraction, which is a more profound thing and has not yet been entirely explained. Attraction is a mystery in which a secret chemistry is involved, ranging from the temperature of her skin to the gleam of his eyes, from the firmness of her breasts to the taste of his lips. "There is no accounting for tastes," the old saying goes; the same is true of love. There are no rules. Attraction is a composite whose nature is subtle and different in every case. It is made up of animal humors and spiritual archetypes, of childhood experiences and the phantoms that people our dreams. Love is not a desire for beauty; it is a yearning for completion. Potions and spells have been a traditional explanation of the strange, involuntary nature of amorous attraction. All peoples have legends about this kind of magic. In the West, the best-known example is the story of Tristan and Isolde, tirelessly repeated in art and poetry. In the Spanish theater Celestina's powers of persuasion do not lie solely in her eloquent language and treacherous flatteries but also in her philters and potions. Although the idea that love is a magic lasso that literally captures the will of the lover goes very far back in time, it is an idea that still lives: love is a magic spell, and the attraction that unites the lovers is a bewitchment. What is extraordinary is that this belief coexists with its opposite: love is born of a free decision, the voluntary acceptance of fate.

WITHOUT GIVING UP the magic philter of Tristan and Isolde, the Renaissance and Baroque conceived a theory of passion. The favorite symbol of the poets of this period was the irresistible magnet. Two legacies of Greco-Roman antiquity were influential here: the theory of the four humors and astrology. Affinities and repulsions between the sanguine, nervous, phlegmatic, and melancholy temperaments explained erotic attraction. The four-humor theory had its origins in the medical tradition of Galen and also in Aristotle, to whom a treatise on the melancholy temperament was attributed. The belief in the influence of the stars originated in Babylon, but the version adopted by the Renaissance has Platonic and Stoic roots. According to *Timaeus*, as souls descend to earth to be incarnated in a body, they receive the auspicious and inauspicious influences of Venus, Mars, Mercury, Saturn, and the other planets. These influences determine one's predispositions and inclinations. The Stoics viewed the cosmos as a system ruled by the antipathies and sympathies of the universal energy (*pneuma*), which were reproduced in each individual soul. In both doctrines the individual soul was part of the universal soul and moved by the forces of attraction and repulsion that moved the cosmos.

THE ROMANTICS AND the moderns replaced Renaissance Neoplatonism with various psychological and physiological explanations, yet for them love remained an inescapable fate. Except that this fate, whether its victims are Calixto and Melibea in the Renaissance or Hans Castorp and Claudia in Thomas Mann's *Magic Mountain*, is gladly embraced, ardently invoked and desired. Fate is manifested only through

the complicity of our freedom. The nexus between freedom and destiny—in Greek tragedy and the Hispanic
religious plays, the *autos sacramentales*—is the focal
point around which all lovers revolve. When we fall in
love, we choose our fate. Whether it be love of God or
love of Isolde, love is a mystery in which free will and
predestination intertwine. But the dark side of freedom
also grows in the psychic subsoil: the poisonous vegetation of infidelities, betrayals, abandonments, forgetfulness, jealousy. Love's freedom and its alternately
light and dark flowers have been the central subject of
our poets and artists. Of our lives as well, our real life
and our imaginary life, the life we live and the life we
dream.

THE FIFTH ELEMENT of our idea of love consists,
like the others, in the indissoluble union of two con-
traries, the body and the soul. Our tradition, from Plato
on, has exalted the soul and scorned the body. But
from its very beginnings love has ennobled the body:
without physical, carnal attraction there is no love.
Today we are witnessing a radical rejection of Platonism. Our era rejects the soul and reduces the human
mind to a reflex of bodily functions. Thus the concept
of the person, a twofold inheritance from Christianity

and Greek philosophy, is profoundly undermined. The concept of the soul is the basis for the concept of the person, and without a person love regresses to mere eroticism. I will return to the twilight of the concept of the person in our society; for the time being I limit myself to saying that it has been the principal reason for the political disasters of the twentieth century and of the general debasement of our civilization. There is a close, causal, necessary connection between the concepts of the soul, the person, human rights, and love. Without the belief in an immortal soul inseparable from a mortal body, neither the exclusive nature of love nor its consequence—the transformation of desired object into desiring subject—could have arisen. In short, love demands as its prerequisite the concept of the person, and the concept of the person requires a soul incarnated in a body.

The word *person* is of Etruscan origin and in Rome designated the mask of an actor on the stage. What lies behind the mask, what is it that *animates* the character? The human mind, soul, or spirit. The person is a being made of a soul and a body. And here is another great paradox of love, perhaps the central one, its tragic nexus: we simultaneously love a mortal body, a body subject to time and its accidents, and an immortal soul.

The lover loves the body and the soul in equal measure. It can even be said that were it not for the attraction of the body, the lover would be unable to love the soul that animates it. For the lover the desired body is a soul, and he speaks to it in a language beyond language, a language comprehensible not through the faculty of reason but through the body, through the skin. And the soul is palpable: we are able to touch it; its breath cools our eyelids or warms the nape of our neck. Everyone in love has felt this shift of the physical into the spiritual and vice versa. Everyone knows it with a knowledge that rebels against reason and language. In his "Second Anniversary," John Donne tells us:

> . . . her pure and eloquent blood
> Spoke in her cheekes, and so distinckly wrought
> That one might almost say, her bodie thought.

Seeing in the body the attributes of the soul, those in love fall into a heresy anathematized by both Christians and Platonists. It was considered an aberration, even a madness: the *mad love* of the medieval poets. Love is mad because it traps lovers in an insoluble contradiction. Within the Platonic tradition, the soul lives as a prisoner of the body; within the Christian tradition, we come into this world only once and only to save our soul. In both cases there is an opposition between soul and body, despite the fact that Christianity has mitigated it through the dogma of the resurrection of the flesh and the doctrine of glorious bodies. But love is a transgression of both the Platonic and Christian traditions, for it transfers the attributes of the soul to the body, which then ceases to be a prison. The lover loves the body as if it were the soul and the soul as if it were the body. Love commingles heaven and earth: that is the great subversion. To say, "I love you forever," confers on an ephemeral and ever-changing creature two divine attributes: immortality and immutability. The contradiction is truly tragic: the flesh undergoes corruption, and our days are numbered. Nonetheless, we love. We love with body and soul, in body and soul.

THIS DESCRIPTION OF the five elements that make up our image of love, however superficial it may be, does seem to demonstrate love's contradictory, paradoxical, mysterious nature. I discussed five, but they can be reduced to three: exclusivity, which is love for only one person; attraction, which is one's fate freely accepted; the person, who is a soul and a body. But these elements cannot be separated; they exist in constant struggle and reconciliation with themselves and with others. Contrary, as though they were the planets of a strange solar system of the passions, they revolve around a single sun. This sun, too, is twofold: the couple. There is continual transmutation of each element: freedom chooses servitude, fate becomes choice, the soul is body and the body soul. We love a mortal being as though he or she were immortal. Lope said it better: "To call what is eternal temporal." Yes, we are mortal, we are the children of time, and no one is spared death. We know not only that we will die but that the person we love will die. We are the playthings of time and accident; sickness and old age disfigure the body and cause the soul to lose its way. But love is one of the answers that humankind has invented in order to look death in the face. Through love we steal from the time that kills us a few hours which we turn now into paradise and now into hell. In both ways time expands and ceases to be a measure. Beyond happiness or unhappiness, though it is both things, love is intensity: it does not give us eternity but life, that second in which the doors of time and space open just a crack: here is there and now is always. In love, everything is two and everything strives to be one.

1. *Le lys dans la vallée.*

2. *Nichomachean Ethics*, VIII.

3. The Yuan Pass, beyond the city of Wei, was the last military post on the border of the territory of the barbarians (*Hsieng-nu*).

4. Michel de la Montaigne, "On Friendship," *Essays*, I, 28.

5. See *Sor Juana o Las trampas de la fe*, 128–134, vol. 5 of my *Obras Completas*.

The Morning Star

FROM THE SEVENTEENTH century on, Europeans have been examining and judging themselves. This inordinate interest in self is not merely narcissism: it is anguish in the face of death. The Greeks, at the zenith of their civilization, invented tragedy; they invented it, Nietzsche said, because of an excess of well-being. Only a strong and lucid organism can look directly at the cruel sun of destiny. Historical awareness was also born as the West was born, and he who says the word *history* says awareness of death. And modernity—the heir of Christianity, which invented the examination of conscience—has invented criticism. Criticism is one of the things that distinguish us from other periods; neither antiquity nor the Middle Ages engaged in it with anything like the passion modernism has shown: criticism of others and of ourselves, of our past and of our present. The examination of conscience is an act of solitary introspection, but in it the phantoms of others appear, as well as the phantom of what we once were—a plural phantom, since we have been many. We make this descent into the cave of our conscience, filled with the idea of death: we descend toward the past because we know that one day we will die, and before we do, we wish to be at peace with ourselves. I believe that something similar can be said of philosophical-historical reflections on Western civilization: they are examinations of conscience—a diagnosis of the health of our society and a discourse in the face of its more or less imminent death. From Vico to Valéry our philosophers have not ceased to remind us that civilizations are mortal. In the last fifty years this melancholy exercise has become more and more frequent: almost always admonitory and sometimes despairing. There are very few philosophers today, whatever their persuasion, who dare to proclaim the advent of a "bright morning." If we think in historical terms, we live in the age of mud.

Studies of the historical and moral health of our society include the sciences and various subjects: economics, politics, law, natural resources, diseases, demography, the general decline of culture, the crisis in the universities, ideologies—in short, the entire range of human activity. In none of these studies, however—the exceptions can be counted on one's fingers—is there the slightest mention of love, its history in the West and its present situation. I am referring to books and studies on love properly speaking, not to the abundant literature, from essay to treatise, about human sexuality, its history and anomalies. Love is another matter, and its omission says a great deal about the frame of mind of our era. If the study of political and religious institutions, economic and social patterns, philosophical and scientific ideas is indispensable for an understanding of what our civilization has been and is, why shouldn't the same be true of the study of our feelings, among them the one which has been the center of our emotional life, both imaginary and real, for a thousand years? The demise of our image of love would be a greater calamity than the collapse of our economic and political systems: it would be the end of our civilization. That is, of the way we feel and live.

But we should correct the habit of thinking only in

terms of Western civilization. Although we are witnessing the resurrection of national and even tribal particularism in many parts of the world today, it is clear that for the first time in the history of our species we are living in a global society. Western civilization has spread to the entire planet. In the Americas it destroyed native cultures; we in the Americas are an eccentric dimension of the West. Its continuation and replica. The same can be said of the peoples of Oceania and Africa. I am not dismissing native societies and their works; I am merely stating a fact. Predicting the return to African cultures or to Tenochtitlán or the Inca empire is a sentimental aberration—worthy of respect but mistaken. Or else it is an act of cynical demagoguery. The influence of the West has been decisive in the East also. I scarcely need remind my readers of the numerous and profound similarities between our concept of love and those of the Orient and India. In the case of Islam the relationship is closer still: courtly love is unthinkable without Arabic eroticism. Civilizations are not fortresses but crossroads, and our debt to Arabic culture in this respect is immense. In short, the image-idea of love today is universal, and its fate, at this end of the century, is inseparable from the fate of world civilization.

Let me repeat that I am not speaking of the feeling of love, which belongs to all times and places, but to the concepts of it that have been developed by societies. These concepts are not logical constructions; they are the expression of deep psychological and sexual aspirations. Their identity is not a product of the rational mind but of life. It is for this reason that I call them images. I add that if they are not a philosophy, they are a vision of the world, and therefore they are also an ethic and an aesthetic: a *courtesy*. The remarkable continuity of the image of love from the twelfth century to our own day does not mean immobility. On the contrary, its history is rich in change and innovation. Love has been a constantly creative and subversive sentiment.

Love has been, for good and for ill, the most changeable in the West. Think, for example, of the institution of marriage: from a religious sacrament to an interpersonal contract, from an arrangement between families to an agreement between individuals, from dowries to separate bank accounts, from an indissoluble, lifelong bond to modern divorce. Or consider adultery. Today we are far indeed from seventeenth-century husbands slitting their wives' throats to preserve their honor. It is not necessary to catalog all the changes. The great novelty of our century is the moral loosening of the liberal societies of the West. In my opinion, this is explained by the conjunction of three factors. The first factor, a social one, has been the increasing independence of women. The second is technological: the invention of contraceptive devices that are more effective and less dangerous than those of earlier times. The third factor belongs to the realm of beliefs and values: the change in status of the body, which has ceased to be the inferior, perishable, and purely animal half of a human being. The revolution of the body has been and is all-important in the twofold history of love and eroticism: it has freed us, but it can also degrade and debase us. I will come back to this subject.

Literature portrays the changes of society. It also paves the way for them and prophesies them. The gradual crystallization of our image of love has been the work of changes not only in mores but also in poetry, the theater, and the novel. The history of love is the history of a passion but also of a literary genre—of the images that writers give us. These images have been portraits, transfigurations, copies of reality, or visions of other realities. Literature in turn has received sustenance from philosophy and the thought of each era: Dante learned from Scholasticism, the Renaissance poets from Neoplatonism, Laclos and Stendhal from the

Encyclopédie, Proust from Bergson, modern poets and novelists from Freud. In Spanish the best example in this century is the work of Antonio Machado, a poet-philosopher whose work revolves around human temporality and our essential "incompleteness." His poetry, as he himself once said, is a "borderline song"—on the other side lies death—and his thoughts about love are a meditation on the absent beloved, on absence itself.

I am persuaded that it is no exaggeration to say— not as though this were a historical law, yet it is more than a coincidence—that all the great changes in love correspond to literary movements. Literature prepares the way for them, reflects them, converts them into high ideals. Provençal poetry offered the feudal society of the twelfth century the image of courtly love as a life worthy of imitation. The figure of Beatrice, the intermediary between this world and the other, gave rise to a series of such creations, which includes Goethe's Marguerite and Nerval's Aurelia; at the same time it brought light and solace to the nights of many loners. Stendhal described love-passion "scientifically" for the first time. I put scientifically in quotes because his description is more in the nature of a confession than a theory, although codified by eighteenth-century thought. The Romantics taught us how to live, die, dream, and, above all, how to love. Poetry has exalted love, analyzed it, re-created it, and offered it as a model for universal imitation.

THE END OF World War I affected every walk of life. The freedom in manners and morals, especially sexual, was unprecedented. In order to understand the joy of the young people and the daring behavior of those years, we must remember the strictness and prudery that throughout the nineteenth century imposed middle-class morality on the world. After the war women came out onto the street, bobbed their hair, raised the hems of their skirts, showed their bodies, and stuck out their tongues at bishops, judges, and teachers. Erotic liberation coincided with artistic revolution. In Europe and America there suddenly appeared great poets of modern love—a love that commingled body and mind, rebellion of the senses and of thought, freedom and sensuality. It was the eruption of the buried language of passion. The same thing happened in Russia before the leaden age of Stalin descended upon that country. But none of these poets left us a theory of love similar to that given us by the Neoplatonists of the Renaissance or by the Romantics. It was religion and politics that interested Eliot and Pound, not love. As in the twelfth century, the exception was France. There the aesthetic avant-garde, Surrealism, soon turned into a philosophical, moral, and political rebellion that had eroticism as one of its focal points. The best Surrealist poetry is love poetry; I am thinking especially of Paul Éluard. Some of the Surrealists also wrote essays; in a beautiful essay Benjamin Péret coined the expression "sublime love" to differentiate the sentiment from Stendhal's love-passion.[1] And the tradition begun by Dante and Petrarch was continued by the central figure of Surrealism, André Breton.

In Breton's work and life, reflection and combat are commingled. If his philosophical temperament placed him within the lineage of Novalis, his audacity led him to fight in the *militia amoris* like Tibullus and Propertius, not as a private but as a captain. From the beginning, Surrealism presented itself as a revolutionary movement. Breton wanted to conjoin the private and the social, the rebellion of the senses and heart—embodied in his idea of exclusive love—and the social and political revolution of Communism. He failed to accomplish this, and there are echoes of that failure in the pages of *L'amour fou*, one of the few modern books that deserve to be called electric. His contempt for bourgeois morality was intransigent. The Romantics, fighting the taboos of their society, had been the first to herald free love. Although in the Europe of the 1920s and 1930s many taboos still existed, the doctrine of free love had been accepted in certain groups and milieus. There, promiscuity reined, disguised as freedom. Breton's battle for love took place on three fronts: he opposed the Communist determination to ignore private life and its passions; he opposed the old prohibitions of the Church and the bourgeoisie; and he opposed those who were "emancipated." Fighting the first two was not difficult, intellectually speaking; fighting the third group was difficult, for it implied a criticism of the liberty of libertarians.

One of Breton's great merits was that unlike most of his contemporaries he understood the subversive role of love—of love, not only of eroticism. He also perceived, though not clearly, the differences between love and eroticism, but was unable or unwilling to probe deeper into those differences, and so he missed the chance to give his idea of love a more solid foundation. In his attempt to incorporate that idea into the revolutionary movement of his time—did he know this?—he was following the poets of the past, especially Dante, one of the founders, who had tried to abolish the opposition between courtly love and Christian philosophy. In

Breton the duality of Surrealism once again manifests itself: it was a subversion, a rupture, yet at the same time it continued the central tradition of the West, that current which periodically seeks to unite poetry and thought, criticism and inspiration, theory and action. In the days of the great moral and political disintegration that preceded World War II, it was exemplary of Breton to proclaim the cardinal place occupied by exclusive love in our lives. No other poetic movement of this century has done so, and therein lies the superiority of Surrealism—not an aesthetic superiority, a spiritual one.

BRETON'S POSITION WAS subversive and traditional. He was opposed to the prevailing morality in circles both bourgeois and pseudorevolutionary; but with the same resolve he continued the tradition begun by the Provençal poets and passed on by the Romantics. To lend his support to the idea of exclusive love in the very days of the great erotic liberation that followed World War I was to expose himself to the derision of many; but with courage and intelligence Breton dared to defy avant-garde opinion. He was not an enemy of the new erotic freedom, but he refused to confuse it with love. He pointed out the obstacles that stand in the way of love as a free choice: the moral and social prejudices, class differences, alienation. This last seemed to him to be the major obstacle: How to choose, if we are not masters even of our own selves? Following Marx, Breton attributed alienation to the capitalist system; when capitalism disappeared, alienation would disappear. His other great teacher, Hegel, the first to formulate the concept of alienation, held a less optimistic view. Alienation is the feeling that we are absent from ourselves; other powers (phantoms?) displace us, usurp our true self, and make us live a substitute life. Not being what one is, being outside oneself, being a faceless, anonymous other, an absence: this is alienation. For Hegel alienation comes from *excision*.

What did Hegel mean by excision? Kostas Papaionnou explains: "The Judeo-Christian concept devalued nature and transformed it into an object. . . . At the same time it broke the organic tie between man and the City (Polis). Lastly, modern reason generalized excision: having placed spirit and matter, soul and body, faith and understanding, freedom and necessity in opposition, excision finally encompassed all oppositions within one: *absolute subjectivity and absolute objectivity*."[2] But there is a farthest point in this separation of oneself from the world, after which man "tries to make his

way back to himself, and salvation becomes accessible."
Like all his generation, Hegel initially believed in the
French Revolution and thought that it would do away
with alienation and reconcile human beings with nature
and with themselves. The failure of the revolution
obliged him to retreat and conceive a philosophy that
would reconstruct a totality from the fragments to
which ceaseless negativity had reduced it. Instead of the
incomplete healing of the excision that the French Revolution represented, Hegel proposed a philosophy that
answered the enigma of history and gave a diagnosis of
the excision. Not a "philosophy of history" but a "philosophical history" of humankind. Since civil society had
proved "incapable of serving as a universal subject, it
ought to subordinate itself to the State. . . . If the Polis
was impossible, then the State would be transcendent
in relation to society." A healing of the excision and of
alienation? Yes, but at the expense of the subject, gob-
bled up by the state, which to Hegel was the highest
form the objective spirit could take.

Perhaps the error of Hegel and his disciples lay in
their seeking a historical, that is to say, a temporal, solution to the misfortune of history and its consequences:
excision and alienation. The calvary of history, as he
called the historical process, is experienced by a Christ

who endlessly changes countenance and name yet is the same: human. Humankind is the same, but it is never *situated* within itself: it is time, and time is constant separation from self. The existence of time can be refuted and regarded as an illusion, which is what the Buddhists did. But they were unable to escape its consequences: the wheel of reincarnations and karma, the guilt of the past that ceaselessly impels us to live. We can deny time but cannot avoid its embrace. Time is a continual excision, and it never rests: it reproduces itself, multiplying as it withdraws from itself. Excision is not healed by time but by something or someone representing nontime.

Each minute is a knife blade of separation: How to trust our life to the blade that may slit our throat? The remedy lies in finding a balm that heals forever the wound inflicted upon us by time's hours and minutes. Ever since it appeared on earth, the human being has been incomplete whether because it had been driven out of paradise or because it is a passing stage in the evolution of life. Almost from the moment of birth, humans flee from themselves. Where do they go? In endless search of themselves. A human being is never what he is but the self he seeks. Once he catches up with himself or believes that he has, again he separates himself, leaves himself behind, continues his pursuit. He is the child of time. And time is his essence and his infirmity. The cure lies only outside time. And if there is nothing or no one outside time? Then he is doomed and forced to live with the terrible truth. The balm that heals the wound of time is called religion; the knowledge that we must live for a lifetime with our wound is called philosophy.

Is there no way out? Yes, there is: at certain moments time opens just a crack and allows us to glimpse *the other side*. These moments are experiences of the merging of subject and object, of *I am* and *you are*, of now and forever, here and there. They are irreducible to concepts, and we can express them only through paradox and the images of poetry. One of these experiences is love, where sensation merges with sentiment and the two with spirit. It is the experience of complete otherness: we are outside ourselves, hurtling toward the beloved. And it is the experience of the return to our origin, to the place that does not exist in space and is our native land. The beloved is, then, both terra incognita and the house where we were born, what is unknown and what is recognized. It is helpful here to quote not a poet or mystic but a philosopher such as Hegel, the great master of oppositions and negations.

In one of his juvenilia he says: "Love excludes all oppositions and hence it escapes the realm of reason. . . .
It makes objectivity null and void and hence goes beyond reflection. . . . In love, life discovers itself in itself,
devoid now of any incompleteness." Love does away
with excision. Forever? Hegel does not say, but in his
youth he probably believed so. It may even be said that
his entire philosophy and in particular the mission he
assigns to dialectics—an illusory logic—is simply a gi-
gantic translation of this youthful vision of love into the
conceptual language of reason.

In the same text Hegel sees with extraordinary depth
the great and tragic paradox that is the basis of love:
"Lovers can separate from each other only to the degree
that they are mortal or when they reflect on the possibility of dying." In fact, death is the force of gravitation of love. The amorous impulse uproots us from
the earth and from the place where we are; the awareness of death causes us to fall—we are mortal, we are
made of earth, and to earth we must return. I venture
to say something more. Love is life to the full, at one
with itself: the opposite of separation. In the sensation
of the carnal embrace the union of the couple becomes
feeling, and feeling in turn becomes awareness; love is
the discovery of the unity of life. But in that instant the

compact unity is broken in two, and time reappears: it is a great hole that swallows us. The double face of sexuality reappears in love. An intense appetite for life and the extinction of that appetite, the two as one. The ascent is a descent, the tension a relaxing. And thus total fusion includes the acceptance of death. Without death, life—ours, here on this earth—is not life. Love does not vanquish death but makes it an integral part of life. The death of the loved one confirms our doom: we are time, nothing is permanent, and living is a continual separation. And yet time and separation also come to an end in death: we return to the featurelessness of the beginning, to that state of which we catch a glimpse in carnal copulation. Love is a return to death, to the place of reunion. Death is the universal mother. "I shall mix the dust of your bones with the dust of mine," Cynthia says to her lover. I agree that Cynthia's words cannot satisfy Christians or anyone else who believes in another life after death. Still, what would Francesca have said had someone offered to save her but not Paolo? I am of the opinion that she would have answered: To choose heaven for myself and hell for my beloved is to choose hell, to seal my doom twice over.

BRETON ALSO CONFRONTED the other great mystery of love: choice. Exclusive love is the result of choice, but is not choice in turn the result of a series of circumstances and coincidences? And are these coincidences mere chance, or do they have a meaning and obey a hidden logic? Such questions kept Breton awake at night and led him to write memorable pages. The meeting of those who become lovers precedes choice, and even in the meeting chance appears to be the determining factor. Breton argued that the meeting follows a series of events that have no plan and are independent of our will. I walk aimlessly down a street and come upon a passerby; her face appeals to me; I want to follow her, but she disappears around a corner. A month later, at the house of a friend or on leaving a theater or entering a café, I see the woman again. She smiles, I speak to her, she answers, and so begins a relationship that will mark both of us forever. There are a thousand variations of the meeting, but in all of them an agent intervenes that at times we call chance, at times fate or predestination. Whether chance or fate, this series of objective events crosses the path of our subjectivity, inserts itself in it, and assumes the dimension of what is most intimate and powerful in each of us: desire. Breton brought this phenomenon to the attention of Engels and called the intersection of the two series, the outer and the inner, "objective chance."[3]

Breton defines objective chance as "a form of outer

necessity that opens a path into the human uncon-scious." The outer cause intersects with an inner cause: the unconscious. Both are outside our will, both determine us, their conjunction creating order, a tissue of relations, and we are ignorant of the end result and of their reason for being. Is the chain of circumstances accidental, or does it have a meaning, a direction? In either case we are the playthings of alien forces, instru-ments of a fate that assumes the paradoxical and con-tradictory form of a necessary accident. In Breton's mythology, objective chance fulfills the function of the magic philter in the legend of Tristan and Isolde, and of the magnet in the metaphors of Renaissance poetry. Objective chance creates a literally magnetized space: the lovers, like sleepwalkers possessed of second sight, wander about, meet each other, and become joined. Breton re-creates with poetic clairvoyance those states that all lovers are aware of at the beginning of their relationship, aware that they stand at the center of a tissue of coincidences, signs, and correspondences. However, he warns us repeatedly that he is not writing a novelistic tale or a fiction: he is presenting us with a document, giving us an account of a true experience. The fantasy and uncanniness are not the author's in-ventions: they are reality itself.

Objective chance, as Breton sets it forth, is presented as another explanation of the mystery of amorous attraction. Like the love potion, the influence of the stars, or the childhood tendencies of psychoanalysis, it leaves intact the other mystery: the conjunction of fate and freedom. But whether the relationship is the result of accident or predestination, to reach fulfillment the complicity of our will is required. Love, any love, implies a sacrifice; and we choose that sacrifice without batting an eye. This is the mystery of freedom, as the Greek tragedians, Christian theologians, and Shakespeare saw with such clarity. And for Dante and Cavalcanti love was an accident which our freedom transformed into a choice. Cavalcanti said: Love is not virtue, but having been born of perfection (of the beloved), it is what makes virtue possible. I should add that virtue, no matter what meaning we attribute to the word, is first and foremost a *free act*. In short: love is freedom personified, freedom incarnated in a body and a soul.

With Breton the period before World War II comes to an end. The tension that runs through his pages was probably generated by the awareness that he was writing as night was about to fall: in 1937 the clouds of war that had darkened the Spanish sky were gathering in his sky. Despite his revolutionary fervor, did he think that his testimony was also a testament, a legacy? I don't know. In any event, he realized how precarious and elusive are the ideas with which we attempt to explain the mystery of love. A mystery that is part of a greater one: the human being, who, suspended between chance and necessity, transforms his predicament into freedom.

THE ANCIENTS REPRESENTED Venus, the morning star, by the figure of a youth bearing a torch. Translating a passage of the Gospels where Jesus speaks of Satan as "a spark fallen from heaven," St. Jerome used the word that designated the morning star: Lucifer. Lucifer (*lux, lucis*: light + *ferre*: to bear). A felicitous shift of meaning: to call the rebellious angel, the most beautiful one of the heavenly army, by the name of the herald that announces the first light of dawn was an act of great moral and poetic imagination. Light is inseparable from shadow, flight from fall. In the center of the total darkness of evil a hesitant reflection appeared: the dim light of dawn. Lucifer—beginning or fall, light or shadow? Perhaps both. Poets appreciated this ambiguity, and we know the advantage they took of it. Lucifer fascinated Milton and the Romantics, who turned him into the angel of rebellion and the torchbearer of freedom. Mornings are short, and those illuminated by the light of Lucifer are shorter still. That light appeared at the dawn of the eighteenth century, and its reddish splendor faded in the middle of the nineteenth, although it continued to illumine the long dusk of Symbolism with a tenuous and pearly light, a light of thought rather than of the heart. Toward the end of his life Hegel conceded that philosophy always arrives too late and that the light of dawn is followed by twilight: "The owl of Minerva takes wing at dusk."

Modernity has had two mornings: the one lived by Hegel and his generation, which begins with the French Revolution and ends fifty years later; and the one that begins with the great scientific and artistic awakening that preceded the first great war of the twentieth century and ended with the outbreak of the second. The emblem of this second morning is, again, the ambiguous figure of Lucifer. The anger of evil—his shadow —engulfs both wars, and Hitler's and Stalin's camps, and the bombing of Nagasaki and Hiroshima. And his is the spark—he the rebel angel of light—that kindles all the great innovations of our era in science, ethics, and the arts. From Picasso to Joyce and from Duchamp to Kafka, the literature and art of the first half of the twentieth century have been Luciferian. The same cannot be said of the period that followed World

War II, the last stages of which period, according to all the signs, we are still living through. The contrast is striking. Our century began with great revolutionary movements in the domain of art, such as Cubism and Abstractionism, which were followed by other passionate revolts. Surrealism was remarkable for its violence. Every literary genre from the novel to poetry was the scene of successive changes in form and meaning. These changes and experiments also affected works for the stage and films, and they, in turn, influenced poetry and the novel. Simultaneity, for instance, a device in poetry and the novel of those years, is the child of film montage. Nothing like this occurred after World War II. The rebel angel, Lucifer, abandoned the century.

I am neither pessimistic nor nostalgic. The period we are living through is not sterile, even though serious damage has been done to artistic production by the scourges of commercialism, profiteering, and publicity. Painting and the novel, for example, have been turned into products subject to fashion—painting by means of the fetishism of the unique object, the novel by mass production. Nonetheless, since 1950 noteworthy works and personalities have appeared in poetry, music, the novel, and the plastic arts. But no great aesthetic or poetic movement has appeared. The last was Surrealism. We have had resurrections, some brilliant and some merely ingenious. Or, rather, we have had, to use the precise word in English, *revivals*. But a revival is not a resurrection: it is a sudden blaze that soon burns itself out. The eighteenth century had neo-classicism; we have had "neo-Expressionism," a "trans-avant-garde," and even "neo-Romanticism." And what were Pop Art and Beat poetry if not derivations, the former from Dada, the latter from Surrealism? The New York school of Abstract Expressionism was also derivative: it gave us a number of excellent artists but, again, it was a *revival*, a sudden blaze. As much can be said for a postwar philosophical-literary movement which first appeared in Paris and spread throughout the world: existentialism. By its method it was a continuation of Husserl; by its subject, of Heidegger. One more example: from 1960 on, essays and books on Sade, Fourier, Roussel, and others began to be published. Some of these studies are clever, perceptive, at times profound. But they are not original: those authors were discovered forty years before by Apollinaire and the Surrealists. Another revival. There is no point in going on. I repeat: the works of the second half of the twentieth century are different from and even contrary to those of the first half. They are not illuminated by the ambiguous, violent light of Lucifer: they are twilight works. Is the melancholy Saturn our numen? Perhaps, although Saturn is fond of nuance. Mythology paints him as the sovereign of a spiritual golden age whose strength is sapped by black bile, melancholy, a mood partial to chiaroscuro. Our time, by contrast, is simplistic, superficial, and merciless. Having fallen into the idolatry of ideological systems, our century has ended by worshiping Things. What place does love have in such a world?

---

1. "Le noyau de la comète," preface to the *Anthologie de l'amour sublime*, Paris, 1956.

2. Kostas Papaionnou, *Hegel*, Paris, 1962.

3. On the concept of "objective chance" in Breton see the penetrating "Notice" that Marguerite Bonnet devotes to *L'amour fou* in André Breton's *Oeuvres Complètes*, Paris: Bibliothèque de la La Pléiade, Gallimard, 1992, vol. 2. See also, in the same volume, the "Notice" by Madame Bonnet and E. A. Hubert on Breton's *Les vases communicants*. Naturally the expression "objective chance" does not appear in the works of Engels.

The City Square
and the Bedroom

THE COLD WAR lasted more than forty years. In addition to the struggle between the two great blocs that formed after the defeat of the Axis, a polemic tormented the intellectual class and vast segments of opinion. At times that polemic was reminiscent of the theological disputes of the Reformation and Counter-Reformation, or of the violent controversies that led to the French Revolution. There was one important difference, however: the arguments of the Cold War were more political and moral than philosophical and religious; they did not deal with prime or ultimate causes but, rather, had as their principal subject a de facto question: the true nature of the Soviet regime, which claimed it was socialist. A necessary yet arid polemic: it revealed fundamental falsehoods, dishonored many, and hardened the minds and hearts of many, but it did not produce new ideas. It is a miracle that in that bitter atmosphere of quarrels and accusations, of attacks and counterattacks, poems and novels were written, concertos were composed, and canvases painted. No less miraculous was the appearance of independent writers and artists in Russia, Poland, Czechoslovakia, Hungary, Romania, and in other countries made sterile by the double oppression of pseudo-revolutionary dogmatism and the bureaucratic spirit. In Latin America as well, despite military dictatorships and the obfuscation of the majority of our intellectuals, who were enamored of simplistic solutions, a number of remarkable poets and novelists wrote in those years. This era has probably reached its end. An era more of isolated works and personalities than of literary and artistic movements.

In the West the phenomenon that had followed World War I was repeated: a new and freer erotic morality triumphed and became widespread. But this recent period has two characteristics that did not appear before: one, the active and public participation of women and homosexuals; two, the political tone of the demands made by these groups for equality and the recognition of difference. Both demands were and are legitimate; but the guests of Plato's *Symposium*, had they been confronted with them, would have rubbed their eyes: sex a matter for political debate? In the past, eroticism and religion had often been conjoined: Tantrism, Taoism, Gnosticism. But in our time, politics absorbs eroticism and transforms it: it is no longer a passion, it is a right. A gain and a loss: legitimacy is won, but the other dimension, that of passion and spirituality, disappears. During all these years, as I have said, many articles, essays, and books on sexology, sociology, and the politics of sex have been published, all of them foreign to the subject of these reflections. The great absent participant in the revolt of this turn of the century has been love. A situation in sharp contrast to the changes introduced by Renaissance Neoplatonism, the "libertine" philosophy of the eighteenth century, and the Romantic revolution. In what follows I will try to indicate some of the causes of this missing factor, which is a loss that has turned us into invalids—not physical but spiritual invalids.

Ortega y Gasset once pointed out the presence of vital rhythms in societies: periods of the cult of youth followed by periods marked by the veneration of old age; the exaltation of motherhood and the home followed by free love; war and the hunt followed by the contemplative life. I believe that the changes in the collective sensibility we have experienced in the twentieth century follow a pendular rhythm, an oscillation between Eros and Thanatos. When these changes in sentiment coincide with changes in the domain of thought and art, new concepts of love spring up. It is a matter of historical convergence, and courtly love is but one example. The generous and explosive rebellion of 1968 could have been an opportunity to bring about a convergence of this sort. Unfortunately the students' revolt did not possess ideas of its own, nor did it produce original work. Its great merit was to have dared, with exemplary courage, to proclaim and attempt to put into practice the libertarian ideas of the poets and writers of the first half of the century. Sartre and other intellectuals participated in meetings and demonstrations. They were not active participants, however, only a chorus: they applauded but did not provide direction. The events of 1968 were not a revolution; they were the spectacle, the fiesta of revolution. The ceremony was real, but the deity invoked was a ghost. A fiesta in honor of revolution: nostalgia for the Second Coming, a summons of the Absent One. For an instant the ambiguous reddish light of Lucifer flickered, but it soon disappeared from view, obscured by the smoke of controversy in the conclaves of uncompromising and dogmatic young people. Later, some of them formed terrorist gangs.

In the Soviet Union and the countries under its rule, the opposite happened: the old prohibitions became stricter, and in the name of an archaic "progressivism" bureaucracy once again enthroned the most conservative and conventional precepts of nineteenth-century bourgeois morality. Art and literature suffered the same fate: academicism, expelled from Western artistic life by the avant-garde, took refuge in the "land of socialism." The most curious development was to find, among the defenders of mediocre official Soviet culture, many former members of the European and Latin American avant-garde. They never bothered to explain this contradiction to us. And without a word of protest they sanctioned the reactionary legislation of the Communist bureaucracies with regard to sexual and erotic matters. Moral and aesthetic conformism: spiritual abjection.

The Communist empire was a fortress built on quicksand. Some of us believed that the regime was threatened by ossification. No, its malady was a degeneration of the nervous system: paralysis. The first symptoms surfaced at the time of Khrushchev. In less than thirty years the fortress disintegrated and brought down with it an older construction: the czarist empire. The Third Reich was destroyed by Hitler's lack of moderation, Allied bombs, and Russian resistance; the Soviet Union was destroyed by the instability of its foundations—the heterogeneity of the czarist empire, the lack of reality in the Bolshevik social and economic programs, and the cruelty of the methods employed to put them into effect. The rigidity of the doctrine, a simplistic version of Marxism, was a straitjacket forced on the Russian people. The swiftness of the collapse still amazes us. But that great unknown that Russia has been ever since its appearance in history five centuries ago continues. What awaits its people? And what has kept Russia in the world?

The future is impenetrable: this is the lesson we have learned from the ideologies that claimed to hold the keys to history. It is true that at times the horizon is covered with signs—but who can decipher them? Every system of interpretation has failed. We must begin all over again and ask ourselves the question pondered by Kant and the other founders of modern thought. Meanwhile it does not seem rash of me to denounce the superstition of history. It has been and is a great warehouse of novelties, some marvelous and others horrifying; it has also been an immense store-room in which repetitions and cacophonies, disguises and masks pile up. After the intellectual orgies of this century it behooves us to mistrust history and learn to think soberly. An exercise that involves stripping naked: casting aside disguises, tearing off masks. What do they hide? The face of the present? No, the present does not have a face. Our task is precisely to give it one. The present is a material at once malleable and refractory: it seems to obey the hand that sculpts it, yet the result is always different from what we imagined. We must resign ourselves, for there is no other recourse left us: by the mere fact that we are alive, we must confront the present and make out of that confusion of lines and volumes a face. Turn the present into presence. Hence the question about the place of love in today's world is unavoidable and crucial. To make it disappear by sleight of hand is more than an evasion; it is a mutilation.

For many years some of us took part in a battle that often seemed lost: defending the present—formless, imperfect, stained by many horrors but also the seedbed of freedom—from a totalitarian system hiding beneath the mask of the future. The mask finally fell off, and the terrifying face, on contact with the air, began to disintegrate in the same way that, in Poe's tale, Mr. Valdemar's face turned into a grayish liquid. Today the seeds of freedom that we saved from the totalitarianisms of this century are drying up in the plastic bags of democratic capitalism. We must recover them and scatter them to the four points of the compass. There is an intimate, causal relation between love and freedom.

THE HERITAGE THAT 1968 left us was erotic freedom. In this sense the student movement was no prelude to revolution but instead the final consecration of a struggle that began at the start of the nineteenth century, and its groundwork was laid in equal measure by the libertine philosophers and their adversaries, the Romantic poets. But what have we done with that freedom? Twenty-five years after 1968 we realize that we have allowed it to be expropriated by the powers of money and advertising; and we have seen twilight gradually creeping over the image of love in our society. A twofold failure. Once again money has corrupted freedom. I will be told that pornography is a feature of all societies, even primitive ones; it is the natural counterpart of the restrictions and taboos in social codes. As for prostitution, it is as old as the first cities; in the beginning it was associated with temples, as can be seen in the epic of Gilgamesh. Therefore the connection between pornography, prostitution, and money is not new. Images (pornography) and bodies (prostitution) have been, everywhere and always, a commercial product. In that case, where does the novelty of our present situation lie? My answer is, first, that it lies in the proportions the phenomenon has assumed, and, as will be seen, in the qualitative change it has undergone. Second, though it was presumed that sexual freedom would stop the trade in both bodies and erotic images, the truth is that exactly the opposite has occurred. Democratic capitalist society has applied the impersonal laws of the market and the technology of mass production to erotic life. And thus corrupting it, though its success as a business has been enormous.

People have always viewed representations of the human body with a mixture of fascination and fear. Primitive man believed that paintings and sculptures were the magic doubles of real persons. Even today in certain remote corners of the world there are villagers who refuse to allow their photographs to be taken, believing that the person who possesses the image of their body also possesses their soul. In a way they are not mistaken: there is an indissoluble link between what we call the soul and what we call the body. It is odd that in a time when there is so much talk of human rights, it is permitted to rent and sell and place on exhibit images of men's and women's bodies, not excluding their most intimate parts. What is scandalous is not that this is a universal practice accepted by everyone, but that no one is scandalized: our moral instincts have turned numb. In many cultures beauty was seen as a likeness of divinity; today it is a sign used in advertisements. The human image has been considered sacred in all religions and civilizations, and therefore the representation of the body has often been forbidden. One of the great attractions of pornography consisted precisely in the transgression of such a prohibition. And it is here that the qualitative change in pornography has taken place.

Modernity desacralized the body, and advertising has used it as a marketing tool. Each day television presents us with beautiful half-naked bodies to peddle a brand of beer, a piece of furniture, a new model of car, or women's hosiery. Capitalism has turned Eros into an employee of Mammon. Sexual servitude is added to the debasement of the human image. Prostitution is already a vast international network that traffics in all races and ages, not excluding children, as we know. Sade had dreamed of a society with weak laws and strong passions, where the only right would be the right to pleasure, however cruel and lethal it might be. No one ever imagined that commercial dealings would supplant libertine philosophy and that pleasure would be transformed into an industrial machine. Eroticism has become a department of advertising and a branch of business. In the past, pornography and prostitution were handicrafts, so to speak; today they are an essential part of the consumer economy. It is not their existence that alarms me, but, rather, the proportions they have assumed and their nature. Now an institution, they have ceased to be transgressions.

There is no better way to understand our situation than to compare two policies that appear to be totally different yet produce similar results. One is the stupid prohibition of drugs, which, far from eliminating their use, has greatly increased it and made trafficking in them one of the great businesses of the twentieth century; a business so large and so powerful that it defies every police force and threatens the political stability of a number of nations. The other policy is sexual license, sexual permissiveness: it has debased Eros, corrupted the human imagination, desiccated the sensibilities, and made of sexual freedom a mask for sexual servitude. I am not calling for the odious morality of prohibitions and punishments; I am pointing out that the power of money and the profit motive have turned the freedom to love into slavery. In this domain, as in so many others, modern society confronts contradictions and dangers unknown to societies of the past.

The debasement of eroticism corresponds to other perversions that have been and are, I venture to say, the recoil of modernity. It suffices to give a few examples: the free market, which abolished special privileges for the few and discriminatory taxes on sales and imports, still regularly tends to produce huge monopolies that are its negation; political parties, the agents of democracy, have turned into bureaucratic steamrollers and powerful cabals; the media corrupt messages, cultivate sensationalism, hold ideas in contempt, practice a hidden censorship, inundate us with trivial news, and cause genuine information to vanish. How can we be surprised, then, that erotic freedom today represents a form of servitude? I repeat: I am not proposing the suppression of freedoms: I am calling—and I am not the only one to do so—for an end to the usurpation of our freedoms by profiteers. Ezra Pound admirably summed up our situation in three lines:

They have brought whores for Eleusis.

Corpses are set to banquet

at behest of usura.[1]

Death is inseparable from pleasure, and Thanatos is the shadow of Eros. Sexuality is the response to death: cells unite to form another cell and thereby perpetuate themselves. Turned aside from reproduction, eroticism creates a realm apart, ruled by a dual-natured deity: the pleasure that is death. It is no accident that the tales of the *Decameron*, a great glorification of carnal pleasure, are preceded by the description of the plague that devastated Florence in 1348; or that Gabriel García Márquez chose as the setting for a love novel the city of Cartagena in the days of the cholera epidemic. A few years ago AIDS appeared among us with the same silent treachery with which syphilis did earlier.[2] But we are less prepared to confront a deadly epidemic today than we were five centuries ago. In the first place, because of our faith in modern medicine, a faith that borders on superstitious credulity; secondly, because our psychological and moral defenses have weakened. As technology masters nature and separates us from it, our defenselessness against nature's attacks increases. It was a goddess who brought life and death; today it is forces and energy that we can control, channel, and exploit. We ceased to fear nature and believed it was our servant. Suddenly, without warning, it shows us its other face, that of death. We must learn, once again, to look at nature. This calls for a radical change in our attitudes.

I do not know if science will soon find a vaccine for AIDS. I hope so. But what I wish to stress is our psychological and moral vulnerability to this disease. It is clear that prophylactic measures—the use of condoms and other such practices—are indispensable; it is also clear that they are not enough. Contagion is linked to conduct, with the result that the responsibility of each individual plays a role in the propagation of the disease. To ignore this would be hypocritical and disastrous. A specialist writes: "The history of humankind shows that no disease has been successfully eliminated by treatment alone. Our only hope of containing AIDS lies in prevention. Since it is most unlikely that we will have at our disposal in the near future a vaccine that can be administered to the entire population, for the time being the only vaccine that we have available is education."[3] But today our society lacks the moral authority to preach continence, not to mention chastity. The modern state, for good reasons and bad, abstains as much as possible from passing laws on sexual behavior. At the same time family morality, usually closely allied to traditional religious beliefs, has collapsed. Are the media that inundate our homes with sex in any position to propose moderation? As for our intellectuals and thinkers, where among them will we find an Epicurus or a Seneca? There remain the churches. In a secular society like ours, that is not enough. In all truth, besides religious morality, which is unacceptable to many, love is the best defense against AIDS—that is to say, against promiscuity. It is not a physical remedy, not a vaccine; it is a paradigm, a way of life founded on freedom and self-surrender. A vaccine for AIDS will be found someday, but if a new erotic ethics does not come into being, our lack of defense against nature and its immense powers of destruction will continue. We believed we were the masters of the earth and the lords of nature; now we are helpless. In order to recover our spiritual strength we must first recover our humility.

THE END OF Communism forces us to look at the moral situation of our society with greater critical rigor. Its ills are not exclusively economic, but, as always, also political, in the positive sense of the word—that is,

moral. They have to do with freedom, justice, frater-
nity, and, finally, with what we ordinarily call values.
At the center of these ideals is the notion of the person.
The person is the foundation of our political institutions
and our ideas of what justice, solidarity, and social coexistence ought to be. The concept of the person is confused with that of freedom.

It is not easy to define freedom. The subject has been
a matter of debate since the birth of philosophy: What
is the place of freedom in a universe governed by im-
mutable laws? And for those philosophies that allow
contingency and accident, what meaning does the word
freedom have? Between chance and necessity is there a
place for freedom? These questions exceed the limits of
this essay, so I confine myself simply to expressing my
belief. Freedom is not an isolated concept nor can it be
defined in isolation; it is permanently wedded to another concept without which it cannot exist—necessity.
But necessity in turn is impossible without freedom:
each exists only in opposition to the other. The Greek
tragedians saw this with greater clarity than did the
Greek philosophers. Since that time, theologians have
not stopped arguing about predestination and free will.
Modern scientists have returned to the subject, and a
famous contemporary cosmologist, Stephen Hawking,

tells us that black holes represent a physical *singularity*, that is to say, an exception, a place within space-time where the laws of the universe cease to apply. An unthinkable, inconsistent idea. It resembles Kant's antinomies, which he regarded as insoluble. Nonetheless, black holes exist. In like manner then, freedom exists. Knowing that we are setting forth a paradox, we may say that freedom is a dimension of necessity.

Without freedom, what we call a person does not exist. Is there a person without a soul? For most scientists and for many of our contemporaries, the soul has disappeared as an entity independent of the body. Or they regard it as an unnecessary concept. But at the same time that they declare its nonexistence, the soul reappears—not outside the body but precisely inside it. The attributes of what was once considered to be the soul—thought and its faculties, for instance—have become properties of the body. We need only leaf through a treatise on modern psychology and the new cognitive disciplines to note that today the brain and other organs possess nearly all the faculties of the soul. So the body, without ceasing to be a body, has turned into a soul. I will come back to this point. But from a strictly scientific point of view there are still a number of questions that have not been answered. The central one is to explain the leap from neurons to thought. Hegelian logic found an explanation, in all likelihood an illusory one: the dialectical leap from the quantitative to the qualitative. Science, and rightly, is not a supporter of this sort of passkey, but neither has it come up with a convincing explanation of the supposed physiological-chemical origin of thought.

The consequences of this approach have been dismal. The eclipse of the soul has engendered a doubt—a doubt it does not strike me as an exaggeration to call ontological—about what a person really is. Is he or she a mere perishable body, a totality of molecular inter-actions? A machine, as the specialists in the field of artificial intelligence believe? In that case, once we gain the necessary knowledge, we will be able to reproduce it and even improve upon it. A human being, having ceased to be the image and likeness of divinity, now also ceases to be a product of natural evolution and enters the category of industrial production: it is some-thing manufactured. A concept that destroys the notion of the person, and therefore it is a direct threat to the values and beliefs that have been the very foundation of our civilization, of our social and political institu-tions. So the expropriation of eroticism and love by the power of money is only one aspect of the twilight of love: the other is the vanishing of love's constitutive element—the person. The two evils complement each other and open up the perspective of a possible future of our society: technological barbarism.

FROM GRECO-ROMAN antiquity on, despite numerous changes of a religious, philosophical, and scientific nature, we lived in a relatively stable mental universe, for its foundation rested on two apparently immovable pillars: matter and spirit. These two pillars were at once antithetical and complementary. But, from the Renaissance on, they began to totter. In the eighteenth century one of them, spirit, began to fall. Gradually it abandoned heaven and then earth; it ceased to be the first cause, the principle that gives rise to all that exists; it withdrew from the body and from the consciousness. The soul—*pneuma*, as the Greeks called it—is a breath, and once it became no more than a breath, it was a mere puff of wind. Psyche returned to her distant native land, mythology. More and more, through different hypotheses and theories, we make the soul depend on the body, make it one of the body's functions. Meanwhile the other pillar, what the ancients called matter, the extreme limit of the cosmos for Plotinus, has also been falling. It is no longer a substance or anything we can hear, see, or touch; it is energy, which is time and space become each other. The soul is now physical; matter, insubstantial. A double break with tradition that has trapped us inside a sort of parenthesis: nothing we see is real, and what is real is invisible. The ultimate reality not a presence but an equation. The ancients, contemplating the night sky, saw in the constellations an animated geometry: saw order. But for us the universe has ceased to be a mirror or archetype. All these changes have altered the idea of love to the point of making it, like the soul and matter, unknowable.

For the ancients the universe was the visible image of perfection; in the circular motion of the stars and planets Plato saw the very form of being and the good. Reconciliation of motion and identity: the revolutions of the heavenly bodies were not a matter of change and chance but the dialogue of being with itself. Hence the sublunary world, our earth—the realm of accident, imperfection, death—should imitate the celestial order; the society of humankind should pattern itself on the society of the stars. This idea fed the political thought of antiquity and the Renaissance; we find it in Aristotle and the Stoics, in Giordano Bruno and Campanella. The last one to see in the heavens the model of the city of the just was Fourier, who translated Newtonian forces into social terms: in his ideal community, Harmony—passionate attraction, not self-interest— would rule human relationships. But Fourier was an exception; none of the great political thinkers of the nineteenth and twentieth centuries have been inspired by astronomy or physics. The situation was summed up by Einstein: "Politics is for the moment, an equation is for eternity." In other words: the bridge between eternity and time, stellar space and human space, heaven and history has broken down. We are alone in the universe. But for Einstein the universe still possessed a form; it was orderly. Today this belief too is tottering. Modern physics postulates an indeterminate universe, and that universe is expanding, dispersing. Modern society is also dispersing. We human beings are wanderers in a wandering world.

The demise of antiquity's image of the world has its counterpart in the twilight of the idea of the soul. In the sphere of human relations the disappearance of the soul has taken the form of a gradual but irreversible devaluation of the person. Our tradition told us that every man and woman was a unique, unrepeatable being; the modern age sees not beings but organs, functions, processes. The consequences have been awesome. Man is a carnivorous creature and a moral one: like all carnivores, he lives by killing, but in order to kill he needs justification. In the past, religions and ideologies provided him with all sorts of reasons to murder his fellows. The idea of a soul, however, was a defense against murder by states and inquisitions. A feeble, flimsy defense, it will be said. I do not deny it, but add: A defense nonetheless. The first argument in defense of the American Indians, put forth by Spanish missionaries, was to declare that they were creatures with a soul. Who could repeat today, with the same authority, this argument? In the great polemic that deeply touched consciences in the sixteenth century, Bartolomé de las Casas dared to say: We are here in America not to subjugate the natives but to convert them and save their souls. And during the crusades, which justified conquest by conversion of infidels, the notion of a soul was a shield (albeit imperfect) against the greed and cruelty of the advocates of slavery. The soul was the basis of the sanctity and freedom of every person. Because we have a soul, we have free will: the ability to choose.

It has been said that our century can look with scorn on the Assyrians, Mongols, and all the conquerors of history: their massacres were nothing compared to those carried out by Hitler and Stalin. But there has been less discussion of the relationship between the reduction of man to a mechanism and the concentration camps. The totalitarian states of the twentieth century are frequently compared to the Inquisition. The truth is that the Inquisition comes off better: not even in the most somber moments of its dogmatic fury did the Inquisitors forget that their victims were people. Their aim was to destroy their bodies but, if possible, save their souls. I understand that this idea seems horrifying to us, but what of the millions who in the camps of the Gulag lost their souls before they lost their bodies? Because the first thing that was done to them was to turn them into ideological categories—or, rather, to employ the modern euphemism, they were first "expelled from the discourse of history" and then eliminated. "History" was the touchstone: to be outside history was to lose one's human identity. And the dehumanization of the victims corresponded to the dehumanization of the executioners, who saw themselves not so much as pedagogues of the human species as its engineers. Stalin was an "engineer of souls." The words *victim* and *executioner* do not really belong to the vocabulary of totalitarianism, which knew only terms like *race* and *class*— the instruments and agents of a supposed physics of history. The difficulty in defining the totalitarian phenomenon lies in the fact that the old political categories—tyranny, despotism, Caesarism, and so forth—could not be applied to them. Hence the frequent use of *engineer* in the era of Stalin. The reason is clear: the totalitarian state was, literally, the first *soulless* state in human history.

It may seem strange that on speaking of love I find myself in modern political history. The strangeness disappears when one notes that politics and love are the two extremes of human relations: the public and the private, the city square and the bedroom, the group and the couple. Love and politics are two poles joined by an arc: the person. The fate of the person in political society is reflected in his or her love relationship, and vice versa. The story of Romeo and Juliet is unintelligible if the quarrels between the nobles of the Renaissance are not taken into account, and the same is true of the story of Larissa and Zhivago if removed from the context of the Bolshevik revolution and civil war. Love and politics go together throughout the history of the West. In the modern age, since the Enlightenment, love has been a crucial factor in the change in social morality and customs, and in the appearance of new practices, ideas, and institutions. In all these changes—I am thinking above all of two great moments: Romanticism and the period following World War I—the human person was the lever and the axis. When I speak of the human person, I am not evoking an abstraction but referring to a concrete totality. I have used the word *soul* a number of times, and confess that I have been guilty of an omission: the soul, or whatever one chooses to call the human psyche, is not only reason and intellect, it is also a *sensibility*. The soul is bodily: sensation, which becomes emotion, sentiment, passion. The affective element derives from the body, but it is more than physical attraction. Sentiment and passion are the center, the heart of the soul in love. It is as a passion and not merely as an idea that love has been revolutionary in the modern age. Romanticism did not teach us to think; it taught us to feel. The crime of modern revolutionaries has been to reduce the revolutionary spirit to its affective element. And the great moral and spiritual misery of liberal democracies is their affective insensitivity. Money was able to expropriate eroticism because people's hearts and souls had already dried up.

Although love continues to be the subject of twentieth-century poets and novelists, its very heart—the concept of the person—has been wounded. The crisis of the idea of love, the rise of labor camps, and the ecological threat—these are concomitant facts and all closely related to the twilight of the soul. The idea of love has been the moral and spiritual leavening of our societies for a millennium. It was born in a corner of Europe, and like the thought and science of the West it became universalized. Today it is threatened with dissolution. Its enemies are not the age-old ones, the Church and the morality of abstinence, but promiscuity, which turns love into a pastime, and money, which turns love into a form of slavery. If our world is to recover its health, the cure must be twofold. Political regeneration must include the resurrection of love. And both love and politics depend on the rebirth of the concept that has been the focal point of our civilization: the person. I am not thinking of an impossible return to the old notions of the soul, but I believe that under pain of extinction we must find a vision of man and woman that restores to us the awareness of the singularity and identity of both. A vision at once new and old, a vision in which each human being is a unique, unrepeatable, and precious creature. It is incumbent on the creative imagination of our philosophers, artists, and scientists to rediscover not what is most distant but what is most near and everyday: the mystery that each one of us is. To reinvent love, as the poet seeks to do, we must reinvent the human person.

1. Ezra Pound, "Canto XLV" in *Selected Poems of Ezra Pound* (New York: New Directions, 1957), p. 137.

2. The majority of specialists today reject the theory of the American origin of syphilis. But it is a fact that Europeans became aware of this disease—probably previously confused with leprosy—after Columbus's voyages. The existence of syphilis in America before the arrival of Europeans is also a proven fact.

3. Mervyn F. Silverman, of the American Foundation for AIDS Research. Cited by Drs. Samuel Ponce de León and Antonio Lazcano Araujo, "Quo vadis Sida?" *La Jornada Semanal* (Mexico City), April 11, 1993.

Digressions on the Way to a Conclusion

IN THE BEGINNING in ancient Greece, the line between science and philosophy was indiscernible; the first philosophers were also, with no discrepancy, physicists, biologists, cosmologists. The best example was Pythagoras: a mathematician and the founder of a philosophical-religious movement. The separation begins a little later, and Socrates completes it: the philosophers' attention shifts toward the inner man. The physical object par excellence was not nature and its secrets but the human soul, the mysteries of consciousness, the passions, and reason. But the interest in *physis* and the cosmos did not decline: Plato cultivated mathematics and geometry; Aristotle studied biology; Democritus, atomism; the Stoics developed a cosmology that has an intriguingly modern aspect. . . . With the end of the ancient world the separation increased. In the Middle Ages the sciences, stagnant, were more practical than theoretical, while philosophy became the servant of the queen of knowledge: theology. In the Renaissance the union of scientific knowledge and philosophical speculation began anew. The alliance was not an enduring one: the sciences gradually won their autonomy, and specialized, each becoming a separate body of knowledge; philosophy, for its part, turned into a general theoretical discourse without empirical basis. The last great dialogue between science and philosophy was that attempted by Kant. His successors engaged in dialogue with universal history (Hegel) or with themselves (Schopenhauer, Nietzsche). Philosophical discourse turned back upon itself, examined and questioned its foundations—the critique of reason, the critique of will, the critique of philosophy, and finally the critique of language. But the areas abandoned by philosophy were gradually taken over by the sciences, from cosmic to inner space, from stars and atoms to cells, and from cells to passions, will, thought.

As the sciences constituted themselves and staked out

the areas of their competence, a twofold process took place. First, the progressive specialization of knowledge; then, in the opposite direction, the appearance of lines of convergence, points of intersection between the various sciences—between physics and chemistry, chemistry and biology. Points where one discipline leaves off and another begins, where exploration requires the cooperation of two or more sciences. In the last half-century this process of intersecting disciplines has accelerated. Time, which once played a secondary role in physics and astronomy, became a crucial factor. Einstein's theory of relativity brought extra motion, so to speak, to Newton's universe, where space and time were invariable. The Big Bang hypothesis (or, as Jorge Hernández Campos calls it in Spanish, the *Gran Pum*) included time in scientific speculation. The universe had a history, and one of the objects of science was to learn that history and render an account of it. Physics became a chronicle of the cosmos. New questions arose: the origin of the universe, its probable end, the direction of the arrow of time—is it obliged to follow the curvature of space and hence return to the point where it started? Such scientific questions are also philosophical. "Contemporary cosmology," a specialist says, "is a speculative cosmology."[1] An intersection, then, of the newest science and the oldest philosophy: the questions scientists are asking themselves today were pondered 2,500 years ago by the Ionic philosophers, the founders of Western thought. But if the questions are the same, is this true of the answers too?

Among the books on the subject that we laymen have been able to read with the greatest benefit is Steven Weinberg's *The First Three Minutes* (1977). Science and history: this book is the most understandable, clearest, and most intelligent account of the three minutes following the Big Bang. Everything that has happened in the cosmos for many billions of years is a consequence of that instantaneous *fiat lux*. But what happened or what existed before then? Like the Bible and other religious and mythological texts, scientists tell us nothing about what came before the beginning. Weinberg says that nothing is known about that and nothing can be said. He is right. But his prudence confronts us with a logical and ontological enigma that has undermined all philosophical certainties: What is nothingness? A contradictory question, one that cancels itself out: it is impossible for nothing to be something, because if it were, it would not be—it would cease to be—nothing. A meaningless question, therefore, the only answer to which is silence . . . which is no answer either.

A safe statement: Nothing can be said about nothing. However, to postulate that nothing, nonbeing, is prior to being—the logical deduction from the Big Bang— is to state something equally contradictory: that nothing is the origin of being. Which leads us directly to the conclusion that is the nonrational, religious foundation of Judeo-Christianity: In the beginning God created the world out of nothing. The religious answer introduces a third enigma, between the enigma that is nonbeing and the enigma that is being: God. But the scientific hypothesis is even more mysterious than the Biblical text: it leaves out the creative agent. I confess that the religious belief strikes me as more reasonable, although it leaves me equally puzzled and unsatisfied: a creative agent, God, who is the supreme being, extracting Himself out of nothingness. From a strictly logical point of view, the scientific hypothesis is less consistent than the religious belief: without an all-powerful creator, how can being emerge from nonbeing? It was with an understandable smile of disbelief that the pagan philosophers greeted the Jewish and Christian idea of a God who makes a world out of nothing. What would their reaction have been to the hypothesis of a universe that bursts forth from nothingness, without cause, impelled by nothing but itself?

In the face of the logical and ontological impossibility

of deducing being from nothing, Plotinus posited a demiurge who mixed together preexisting elements to create, or, more exactly, re-create the world. The demiurge took his inspiration from the ideas and eternal forms. We and the world are copies, likenesses, reflections of eternal reality. Aristotle conceived of an immovable mover, which was a minor contradiction compared to the Biblical account. Perhaps in order to avoid these pitfalls, a number of modern scientists, among them Hawking, suggest that before the Big Bang what would become the universe was a cosmic "singularity," a sort of primordial black hole. Singularities are not governed by the laws of space-time but perhaps are by the principles of quantum physics and the uncertainty principle. The singularities of Hawking and others immediately call to mind the original chaos of Greek mythology. An idea taken up and elaborated on with great subtlety by the Neoplatonists. For Plotinus it was the reverse image of the One: the Many. But just as nothing can be said of the One—not even that it is, since it is located before being and nonbeing—there is nothing that can be said about the Many either, for each property that defines it negates it at the same time. The chaos of Neoplatonism is a superb premonition of the black holes of contemporary physics.

The hypothesis of a primordial singularity is more

consistent than the others: in the beginning there was something—chaos. This idea leads us to another: if the beginning was an exception or singularity (chaos), and if we accept that everything that has a beginning also must have an end, it follows that the universe will eventually return to its original state and become a black hole. The black hole, in turn, reaching some critical mass, may explode in a Big Bang and begin the world all over again. This hypothesis reminds us of the Stoics, who imagined a succession of creations and destructions: from primordial chaos to universe, from universe as a system of attractions and repulsions to a collision that produces a great cosmic blaze, and from this universal fire back to the beginning of the cycle. . . . Thus speculative modern cosmology returns continually, considering the origin of the world, to answers that were given by our philosophical-religious tradition.

With extraordinary effrontery, philosophers have announced the death of philosophy. For Hegel, philosophy was "realized" in his system; for his successor Marx, it was surpassed by dialectical materialism (Engels proclaimed the end of the Kantian "thing-in-itself," reduced to social production through the action of human work); Heidegger accused metaphysics of "hiding being"; others spoke of the poverty of philosophy. To speak of the poverty of science today is equally arrogant.

I do not believe that science is impoverished. I believe the opposite. The great lesson of modern science is precisely in showing us that the questions that philosophy stopped asking itself for two centuries—questions about the origin and the end—are the most important ones. The sciences were obliged to confront these questions sooner or later: it has been a blessing for us that thanks to their prodigious progress, that moment has come in our day. It is one of the few things, in this crepuscular end of the century, that kindles in our spirit a tenuous spark of hope. In 1954, in a letter to a colleague, Einstein wrote: "Physics is no more than a philosophy that takes an interest in particular things; otherwise it would be nothing more than a technique." It might be added that those particular things, after a generation, proved to be fundamental. On another occasion, speaking of himself and his work, Einstein wrote: "I am not really a physicist but a philosopher and even a metaphysician." If that sentence had been written today, Einstein might perhaps have formulated it in a slightly different way: "I am a physicist and for that reason a philosopher and even a metaphysician."

THE QUESTION OF the beginning reappears in the realm of biology. When and how did life begin on earth? Once again, to answer this question the cooperation of different disciplines is necessary: physics, astronomy, geology, chemistry, genetics. Most experts are of the opinion that the appearance on earth of the phenomenon we call life is something of a miracle. By "miracle" they mean that a great number of complex physicochemical and environmental factors had to be present simultaneously in order for life to come about —without the action of an external agent. One of the most famous contemporary geneticists, Francis Crick, who was awarded the Nobel Prize in 1962 for his discovery, with James Watson and Maurice Wilkins, of the molecular structure of DNA, has devoted a book to this subject: *Life Itself, Its Origins and Nature* (1981).[2] Crick begins by telling us that it is almost impossible for life to have originated on our planet: its origin must be sought elsewhere. Where? Not in the solar system, for obvious reasons, but in another system like ours. Crick does not specify the galaxy, does not attempt to locate the place where life originally appeared—that would be impossible—nor does he describe how life could have arisen on that unknown planet. He merely presumes that there, wherever *there* was, conditions were more favorable than on Earth. How, then, did life reach Earth? Owing to the distances that separate suns and galaxies, it would have been impossible for living beings, even if they possessed a life span several times greater than ours, to travel to Earth and plant the first seeds of life. A journey from another galaxy would last thousands of millions of terrestrial years. In 1903, long before Crick, another Nobel Prize winner, Swedish physicist S. A. Arrhenius, was confronted with a similar problem. He came up with an ingenious hypothesis: clouds of floating spores from outer space had fallen on Earth when our globe was what scientists picturesquely call a "broth" favorable to the reproduction of bacteria and other primitive organisms. Arrhenius called his hypothesis Panspermia. Crick took this idea, modified it, and developed it in a curious mixture of logical speculation and fantasy.

Arrhenius's hypothesis had one defect: the tremendous distances and inclemencies of space would have destroyed the clouds of fragile spores long before they could come within range of our planet. Proceeding from one deduction to another, Crick arrived at a logically irreproachable conclusion: the bacteria must have arrived here in hermetically sealed vehicles impervious to meteors, radiation, and other cosmic vicissitudes. From starships we deduce the builders: a civilization at a very high stage of evolution decided to propagate life on the planets of other systems. Crick does not say how these advanced beings knew of the conditions on Earth and the other planets they selected. He reasons that their decision was reached when they discovered that they were doomed to extinction. In an act of cosmic beneficence intended not to save them but life itself, they conceived the idea of transporting the seeds of life to other planets in ships that could endure such a journey. Why bacteria? Because bacteria were the only organisms which, kept in a favorable medium, could reproduce themselves indefinitely and thus survive the interstellar trip. Once on Earth, they would go through the same steps of natural evolution, which eventually would lead to the human species, and a little later to the moment when Crick would write his book and set forth his theory of *directed Panspermia*.

Crick's book is surprising for a number of reasons. Two of them are his deductive rigor and his moral loftiness. But there are inconsistencies, such as the episode of the dinosaurs. Dinosaurs ruled the earth for more than six hundred million years and would still be the dominant species today had it not been for their sudden extinction, which is still unexplained. Some scientists doubt that the cause of their disappearance was the fall of a meteor that darkened the earth, killed the vegetation, and thus deprived them of their food supply.

What would have happened if these great reptiles had not perished? What direction would evolution have taken? The fate of the dinosaurs indicates that the intervention of chance is a fundamental principle in evolution. Their sudden extinction could not be predicted. Thus the appearance of human intelligence on the planet is due to an accident. Biology, like history, cannot be predicted. We are the children of chance.

As in the case of speculative cosmology, it is impossible not to notice the similarity of Crick's ideas, unintended, unconscious, with the hypotheses and doctrines of antiquity on this subject. His extraterrestrial civilization bears more than one resemblance to Plato's Demiurge, and to the various Gnostic sects of the first centuries A.D. The extraterrestrials did not create life—thus Crick gets around the logical difficulty of deriving being from nothing. Like Plato's Demiurge, they use elements that already exist, combine them, and launch them into space; the bacteria descend to Earth like Plato's souls. But there is a substantial difference: the Demiurge does not sacrifice his life for us, whereas the extraterrestrial civilization, on the verge of dying, sends into space its messengers of life. A death that bestows life. The figure of Christ on the Cross is the archetype here, the unconscious model that inspires the fantasy of the dying civilization conceived by Crick. Like so many other scientists, the English biologist forbids himself to introduce a creative agent (God) in order to explain the origin of life on earth, but what is this extraterrestrial civilization that is about to die if not the equivalent of the Christian God and His promise of resurrection? We are in the presence of the translation of a religious mystery into scientific and historical terms.

IN MARVIN MINSKY's *The Society of Mind* (1985), the author does not offer us the apotheosis of an extraterrestrial civilization but that of the electronic engineer. Minsky is one of the experts in the field of artificial intelligence, and he is convinced that the construction of a thinking machine is not only feasible but imminent. His book takes an analogy as its point of departure. What we call mind is a totality of minute parts like the elementary particles that make an atom: electrons, protons, elusive quarks. The forces that move the parts of the mind are not and cannot be different from those that join and separate atomic particles and cause them to move about in space. They are like the circuits that constitute the operation of a huge computer. Another analogy occurs to me: the pieces of a jigsaw puzzle. Individually they have no identifiable form, but when several of them are put together, they become a hand, a leaf, a bit of cloth, until, when all are put together, they acquire a meaning: a girl walking through the woods with her dog. The parts that compose the mind are movable, and like the pieces of the jigsaw puzzle they do not know for what reason or purpose they are moving or who moves them. *They do not think,* although they are components, indispensable components, of thought. Here a difference arises that destroys the symmetry: the puzzle pieces are moved by a hand that knows what it is doing and why. An intention inspires the hand, the head, of the assembler. In the case of the mind there is no assembler: the self disappears. A machine doesn't think, but it *makes* thought even though there is no one guiding it.

One point that Minsky omits: the interaction between the mind, conceived of as an apparatus, and the outside world. In order for the human mind to begin to function—in practice it functions twenty-four hours out of twenty-four, including the time devoted to sleep—it needs to receive an exterior stimulus. The number of these stimuli is practically infinite, so that a thinking machine, in order to choose what interests it, must be provided with a selector of thinkable things

that is the equivalent of what we call sensibility, attention, and will. These faculties are not purely rational;
they are suffused with emotion. Therefore the machine,
in addition to being intelligent, would have to have feelings. It would have to acquire the exact duplicate of
our faculties: will, imagination, understanding, memory, and so on. We thus enter into a repellent fantasy
of a world inhabited by identical creatures. But even if
the thinking machine were a perfect copy of the human
mind, there would in any case be a difference that I do
not hesitate to call immense: the human mind does not
know that it is in reality a machine; it believes in an
illusion—its self, its consciousness. In the case of a machine made by an engineer, what sort of awareness
could it have? Once presented with a stimulus, the
thinking machine begins that series of operations we
call feeling, perceiving, observing, measuring, choosing,
combining, rejecting, trying out, deciding, and so on.
These operations are of a material nature, consisting of
successive conjunctions and separations, juxtapositions
and divisions of the parts that make the machine—until
an idea results, a concept. Plato, Aristotle, Kant, and
Hegel strove to define what an idea and a concept are,
without entirely succeeding. The machine solves the
problem: an idea is a moment in a series of material

operations carried out by minute particles and powered by an electrical current.

Who performs the operations that are the machine's thought? No one. For Buddhists, the self is a mental construct without an existence of its own, an illusion. To suppress it is to suppress the source of error, desire, and misfortune, to free oneself of the burden of the past (karma) and enter the unconditional: total liberation (nirvana). Minsky's thinking machine has no moral or religious concerns: it eliminates the self because the self is unnecessary. But is it really unnecessary? Can we live without the self? For Buddhists, the extinction of the self means the extinction of the illusion we call life, opening for us the doors of nirvana. For Minsky the suppression of the self does not have moral consequences, only scientific and technological ones. The scientific one allows us to understand the functioning of the mind; the technological one will permit us to construct ever simpler, more perfect thinking machines. We must examine this claim more closely.

Ever since humankind began to think, that is to say, ever since we began to be human, a silent witness, consciousness, watches us think, enjoy, suffer, and, in a word, live. What reality does consciousness, the *realization* of what we are doing and thinking, have?

Minsky's idea of consciousness is an image in a mirror. If we look into a mirror, the image we see refers us to our body; but consciousness has no visible shape or form and therefore cannot refer us to a self (considered by Minsky to be an illusion). But neither does it refer to what gave rise to it: the circuitry between the minute particles. If consciousness is the projection of a mechanism, why do that projection and the mechanism itself become invisible? In other words: if I look at myself in a mirror, I see my image; but if I think that I am thinking, or realize what I am doing, I do not see, nor will I ever see, my thoughts. The electrical discharges between the various parts that comprise the mind become invisible, inaudible thoughts that have no location in space. In "The Hollow Men," T. S. Eliot wrote:

> Between the idea
> And the reality
> Between the motion
> And the act
> Falls the Shadow.[3]

In this case, the shadow vanishes: thought has a body but no shadow; it is an anomaly, an authentic singularity, in the meaning that Hawking assigns to the term.

Minsky's thinking machine is presented as a simpler, more economical, and more efficient model of what we call mind or spirit. The truth is that he puts before us a mystery no less formidable than the immateriality of the soul or the transubstantiation of bread and wine in the Eucharist. His machine is miraculous and stupid: miraculous because it produces, with physical means, invisible and unphysical thoughts; stupid because it does not know it thinks them.

Descartes appears to have been the first who conceived the idea of mind as a machine. But a machine guided by a spirit. The eighteenth century saw the universe as a watch wound by an omniscient watchmaker: God. The idea of a machine which functions by itself, which no one controls, and which can increase, decrease, and change the direction of the current that powers it, is a twentieth-century idea. Although this idea, as we have seen, is paradoxical, we cannot dismiss it. It is a fact that we can now build machines capable of carrying out certain mental operations: computers. Although we have not yet built machines that can regulate themselves, specialists in the field say that this will happen in the near future. The questions are: How intelligent can these machines become, and what are the limits of their autonomy? With regard to the first—

Can human intelligence construct objects more intelligent than itself?—the answer is no. For human intelligence to create an intelligence more intelligent than itself, it would have to be more intelligent than itself to begin with. Which is an impossibility at once logical and ontological. As for the second question: human beings are motivated by their desires, ambitions, and plans, but limited by the extent of their intelligence and the means at their disposal. But what can the ambitions and desires of a thinking machine be? Nothing except what is built into it by its constructor: the human being. The autonomy of machines depends, essentially, on humans. A conditional autonomy, therefore, not a genuine autonomy. I return to the comparison between the pieces of a jigsaw puzzle and the parts that make up a thinking machine. The difference between them lies in the fact that an assembler moves the pieces of the jigsaw puzzle, while the parts of the thinking machine are moved by a program activated by an electrical current. What happens if the plug is pulled? The machine ceases to think. The puzzle and machine both depend on an agent. But there is something more: the solution of the puzzle depends on the reassembling of a shape. The assembler has not invented that shape; rather, he reconstructs what is available to him in the form of the various fragmented pieces. In the case of artificial intelligence, something similar takes place: the computer obediently follows a program, a plan created by the operator of the apparatus. So an agent—an ego, a soul, an assembler, a program—is indispensable. But don't the thinking machines that some scientists dream of surpass the limitations of a program? If we are to believe them, such machines will not only have the ability to regulate and control themselves, they will also be much more intelligent than human beings. In a burst of enthusiasm, science-fiction author Arthur C. Clarke recently said: "I consider humans to be a transitory species that will be supplanted by some form of life that includes computer technology." Clarke, like so many others, invokes the spirit of Darwin: thinking machines are a step in natural evolution, just as amoebas, dinosaurs, ants, and human beings were. But there is one great difference: Darwin placed between brackets the notion of a creator, God, who set the process of natural evolution in motion; while Clarke, like Crick and many others, reintroduces the creative agent, who today assumes the persona of biologist or electronic engineer.

Clarke's words represent a widespread way of thinking, especially among scientists and engineers. I was a devoted reader of his books, which are a fascinating synthesis of science and fantasy. With pleasure and nostalgia I remember a sun-filled afternoon more than thirty years ago: I saw him sitting with a friend on the terrace of the Hotel Mount Lavinia, on the outskirts of Colombo. The sea was beating against the shore, covering the cliffs of the tiny bay with a ragged mantle of bubbling foam. I didn't dare to say one word to him: he impressed me as being a visitor from another planet. . . . In the novelist's statement about a new species there reappears, hidden beneath the science, the old speculative spirit that enlivened not only philosophy but also, more frequently, the visions of prophets and founders of religions. Science began by forcing God out of the universe; it enthroned history, embodying it in redemptive ideologies or philanthropic civilizations; today it is replacing these with the scientist-engineer who builds machines more intelligent than their creator and possessing a freedom unknown to Lucifer and his rebel host. The religious imagination conceived of a God superior to his creatures; the technological imagination has conceived of an engineer-God inferior to his inventions.

ALTHOUGH I HAVE my reservations about the modern biological concept of mind, in my opinion it is richer and more fecund than the mechanistic theory, which takes the computer as its point of departure. The biological approach has a more solid basis, since it is founded on the observation of the human organism, that strange and complex composite of sensations, perceptions, volitions, sentiments, thoughts, and actions. Gerald M. Edelman recently published a book that contains a fascinating theory.[4] It not only is a treatise on the neurobiology of the mind, but deals with other subjects as well, such as the rise of consciousness in the course of evolution and the relationships between biological science and physics and cosmology. For Edelman the mind is a product of evolution and thus has a history that goes from atomic particles to cells to thought and its creations. Mind is a characteristic that the human species shares, in rudimentary form, with the mammals, many birds, and certain reptiles.

The existence of intelligent matter on earth is, according to Edelman, a unique phenomenon in the universe. (In this he parts company with Crick.) Neurologist Oliver Sacks has made the following comment on Edelman's book: "We read with excitement the latest theories concerning the mind—whether based on chemistry, quantum theory, or 'computer science'— and then we ask ourselves: Is this all? . . . If we want to have a theory of mind as it really functions in living beings, it must be radically different from any theory inspired by computers. It must be based on the nervous system, on the inner life of the living being, on the functioning of his sensations and intentions . . . on his perception of objects, people, and situations . . . on the ability of superior creatures to think abstractly and share, through language and culture, the awareness of others."[5] In other words, a theory of mind must be rooted in the human being itself, the animal that thinks, speaks, invents, and lives in society (culture). I will comment briefly on some of Edelman's ideas.

The first advantage of Edelman's theory is that it rejects the computer comparison and purely mechanistic explanations as oversimplified. Another advantage is its realism: the mind must be studied precisely in its own medium, the human organism, and as a stage in natural evolution. It is true that the theory is incomplete—there are vast areas yet to be explored—and many of the conclusions lack empirical proof. This does not invalidate its fertility: it is a hypothesis that makes us think. Edelman begins at the beginning, with sensation in its simplest form, which he calls *feelings*: cold or heat, relaxation or tension, sweetness or bitterness. A sensation implies a value judgment: this is unpleasant, this is pleasant, this harsh, and so on, to what is most complex, such as the sorrow that is also joy or the pleasure that is also pain. Sensations are embryonic perceptions, for would we feel if we didn't realize what it was we felt? Perception, therefore, is also conception: when we perceive reality, we immediately impose a form on our perception; we construct it. Every perception is an act of creation.

The idea of the creative nature of perception, Sacks comments, appears earlier, in Emerson. The truth is that its origin goes back to Greek philosophy, and it was common currency in both medieval and Renaissance psychology. It corresponds to the theory, which held sway until the twelfth century, of the function of the so-called "inner senses"—common sense, intuitive judgment, the power of imagination, memory, and fantasy—which were responsible for collecting and purifying the data of the five outer senses and transmitting them as intelligible forms to the rational soul. The image or form that the understanding receives is not the raw data supplied by the senses. The classification of senses also appears in the Buddhist tradition, in a slightly different order: sensation, perception, imagination, understanding. Each designates a step in a process that converts outer stimuli into impressions, ideas, and concepts: perception is already present in sensation, and it is transmitted to the imagination, which passes it along to the understanding, which in turn puts it in a form accessible to the intellect. The creative aspect of mental operations is not a new idea, although the way modern neurology describes it is new.

At each stage of this complicated series of operations—in the network of neurological relations, made up of millions of inputs and responses—an *intention* appears. What we feel and perceive is not simply a sensation or representation but something already endowed with a direction, value, or incipient meaning. Edmund Husserl's phenomenology is founded on the idea of intentionality. He took it, with substantial modification, from Austrian philosopher Franz Brentano. In all our relations with the objective world—sensations, perceptions, images—there is an element without which there can be consciousness neither of the world nor of oneself. An object, the moment it appears in our consciousness, already possesses a direction, an intention. According to Brentano, the subject invariably has an intentional relationship with the object perceived; that is, the object is included in the subject's perception as intentionality. The object, no matter what it is, is desirable or fearsome or enigmatic or useful or already known, and so on.

Edelman argues that the same is true of sensations and perceptions: they are also value judgments. From all of which I would draw this conclusion: the notion of intentionality requires a subject, whether Husserl's consciousness or Edelman's neurological circuitry. Edelman refuses to consider the existence of a subject to whom the object's intentionality can be attributed—and yet he is impressed by "the unity with which the world appears in the eyes of the perceiver, despite the many ways of perceiving it employed by the nervous system." He is no less impressed by the fact that "today's theories of the mind are unable to explain the existence of an element that integrates or unifies all these perceptions."[6] A nearly insoluble dilemma: on the one hand, the negation of the subject; on the other, the need for a subject. How does Edelman resolve it?

He uses a metaphor: the mind is an orchestra that plays without a conductor. The musicians—the neurons and groups of neurons—are connected, and each player responds to the others or seeks their assistance; in this way they collectively create a musical composition. The neurological orchestra, unlike a real one, does not play a score already written; it is constantly improvising. Phrases (experiences) appear and reappear in this improvisation of a symphony that begins in our childhood and ends with our death. Two observations occur to me. The first: in Edelman's hypothesis the initiative passes from the conductor to the players. In the case of a real orchestra, the players are conscious subjects whose intention is to perform together: does that intention also exist in the neurons? If so, have they previously arrived at an agreement? Or is there perchance a preestablished order that governs the neurons' signals for assistance and the responses to them? The conductor thus does not disappear but is distributed throughout the orchestra. The problem is shifted but not resolved. My second observation: improvisation always requires a plan. The example closest to hand is jazz, and the Hindu ragas: the musicians improvise with a certain freedom but within a basic pattern and structure. The same is true of all improvisation, whether musical or not. Be it a battle or a business negotiation, a stroll in the woods or a public debate, we follow a plan. It may have been worked out only a minute before, or be vague and schematic: it is still a plan. And any plan requires a planner. Who drew up the plan for the neurological orchestra?

As we have seen, Edelman does not avoid the difficulty of explaining how the neurons function without a conductor, without a subject. Quite often he refers to the feeling of identity, to a sense of consciousness. These phrases designate *configurations* of neurons. Neurological circuits interconnected throughout our body and made up of millions of neurons (some of which are "nomad tribes," a phenomenon that amazes me and leaves me puzzled) not only build our world with the adobe bricks and the stones of sensations, perceptions, and intellectual concepts, but they also constitute the subject: our being and consciousness. A configuration is both solid and evanescent: it persists yet constantly changes form. There is a continual metamorphosis of our image of the world and of ourselves. This vision— for it is a genuine vision—is reminiscent of the Buddhist idea of the illusory nature of reality and the self. For Buddhists the self does not possess an independent existence: it is a collection of mental and sensory elements. These elements, or aggregates of elements (*skandas* in Sanskrit, *khandas* in Pali), number five in all. They are the components of the self, the product of our karma, the sum total of our errors and faults in our past lives and present one. Through meditation and other means we can destroy ignorance and desire, free ourselves from ego, and enter the unconditional, an indefinable state (nirvana) that is neither life nor death, and concerning which absolutely nothing can be said.

The resemblance between this and the ideas of neu-

rology is extraordinary. The differences are also worthy
of note. The constructor of the self, for the Buddhist,
is karma; for Edelman, the nervous system. Buddhists
must destroy the self if they wish to escape from the
misfortune of birth, breaking the tie that binds the self
to the wheel of incarnations. For Edelman the self and
consciousness are indestructible, barring some grave dis-
ruption of the brain (disease or death). The self, a configuration that depends on interacting neurons, is a
necessary and indispensable artifice; without it we
would be unable to live. Here the great question arises:
On the day humankind learns that its consciousness is
a mere illusion, an artifice, will it be able to go on living
as it has been? This seems impossible. Once consciousness realizes that it is a neural configuration, that its
functioning depends on neurons, it will cease to be consciousness. The concept affects not only the individual
but all society. Our institutions, laws, philosophies,
arts—our entire civilization is founded on the idea of
a human person endowed with freedom. Can a civilization be founded on a neural configuration?

For Buddhists, freedom begins at that moment when
an individual breaks through the crust of his ignorance
and realizes his situation. This *realization* is the result
of a free act: the consciousness decides to dissolve itself

so as to escape the life-death-life cycle. . . . Freedom, like the neurological orchestra, requires a subject, a self. Without a self there is no decision, no freedom, and without freedom there is no human person. Edelman's position in the face of this question is extremely subtle. For him the mind is only "a special kind of process depending on special arrangements of matter." In other words, the matter that constitutes the mind is no different from any other matter; what is unique is its organization. And therefore every mind is different. Each human organism is a collection of subjective experiences, feelings, and sensations (*qualia*); this totality of experiences, though communicable to a certain point through language and other means, is basically an inaccessible domain for other minds.

THE PLURALITY OF minds, Edelman observes, stands in the way of a comprehensive scientific theory; there will always be exceptions, variations, unknown regions. Every scientific description of the mind is doomed to be partial; our knowledge will always be approximate. This truth includes our own inner life: knowing oneself is at one and the same time an unavoidable necessity and an unattainable ideal. Therefore "the problem does not lie in accepting the existence of individual *souls,* since it is clear that each individual is unique and not a machine." The problem lies in "accepting that individual minds are immortal: can an ethic be based on this premise?" I believe it can, and Edelman does also, although he wonders: "What would be the result of accepting that each individual *spirit* is really corporeal and that, precisely for that reason, is mortal, *precious,* and possessed of an unpredictable creativity?" In another passage of his book he suggests that "the new scientific vision of the mind can give new life to philosophy, now free of Husserlian phenomenology, the prolonged fast of science, and the reductiveness of mechanistic theories."

It is impossible not to agree with Edelman. I too believe that "philosophy needs a new orientation." But these statements stand in strange contrast to many of Edelman's basic ideas. To be more precise: they contradict them. Sacks points out that we still cannot see the groups of neurons or map their interactions. Nor can we hear the orchestra that ceaselessly improvises in our brain. Hence Edelman and his colleagues have conceived, as Sacks puts it, "synthetic animals, artifacts that act by means of computers but whose behavior (if this word is applicable) is not programmed or *robotic* but *poetic.*" (Which is a word of Husserlian lineage.) Edelman does not doubt that in a not too distant future it will be perfectly possible to fashion "conscious artifacts." And Sacks comments: "Happily this will not take place until quite far into the next century." Happily? We cannot wash our hands of this matter, putting off to the coming century discussion of so grave a subject. I am amazed and disappointed.

THESE RANDOM REFLECTIONS by a layman on present-day scientific subjects have not been a simple digression: their object was twofold. First of all, to show that contemporary sciences, not out of weakmindedness but, on the contrary, because of the very course of their research, have had to ask themselves philosophical and metaphysical questions that for centuries scientists have ignored, considering them outside their jurisdiction or else superfluous, contradictory, meaningless. The fact that many famous scientists are formulating these questions today indicates that the door is now opened to further discussion on the age-old subject of the relationship between soul and body. I repeat that I am not advocating a return to time-hallowed concepts. Today the body possesses attributes that once were those of the soul, and this is salutary. But the old balance between soul and body has been destroyed. All cultures are familiar with the dialogue—made up of conjunctions and disjunctions—between the body and the nonbody (soul, psyche, atman). Our culture is the first to attempt to do away with this dialogue by suppressing one of the participants: the soul. As I endeavored to show in another text, the body has been increasingly turned into a mechanism, and the same thing has now befallen the soul.[7] The changes in the genealogy of the human being: God's creature in the beginning; later on the result of the evolution of primitive cells; today a mechanism. The disturbing ascendency of the machine as the archetype of the human being puts the future of our species into question.

It seems to me the time is ripe for embarking on a philosophical inquiry, based on contemporary science, that will shed light on the questions that have always been of passionate concern to human understanding: the origin of the universe and of life, our place in the cosmos, the relation between the part of us that thinks and the part that feels, the dialogue between body and soul. All these are closely connected to the subject of this book: love and its place on the horizon of contemporary history.

The second object of my digressions was to show that the social and spiritual malaise of the liberal democra-

cies, described in the previous chapter, has its counterpart in a no less profound malaise in the culture. The
affliction manifests itself in the commercialization of
the arts—painting and the novel in particular—and in
the proliferation of short-lived literary and artistic fashions, which spread as rapidly as medieval epidemics and
leave behind as many victims. In the case of the sciences,
I have discussed above what is of gravest concern:
mechanization, the reduction of complex mental phe-
nomena to mechanical models. The idea of "manufac-
turing minds" leads inevitably to the conveyor belt of
mass production: identical clones of a particular mind.
In accordance with the needs of the economy or politics,
governments or large corporations could order the man-
ufacture of x number of physicians, journalists, teachers,
workers, or musicians. Beyond the dubious practicality
of such an undertaking, it is clear that the philosophy
on which it is based damages the very essence of the
idea of the human person conceived of as a unique and
unrepeatable being. This is what is so disturbing about
the new science, and this is what we must discuss today,
"happily" or not. If a human being is turned into an
object that can be duplicated, then our species becomes
expendable: something for which a replacement can
easily be found, as with any other manufactured

product. The error of this idea is philosophical and moral, and the moral is more serious than the philosophical. The identification of a mind with a machine is not merely an analogy that is perhaps useful from the scientific point of view, but one that carries the risk of terrible abuses. In reality we are confronted with a new variation in a series of attempts at dehumanization that our race has suffered since the beginning of history.

In the sixteenth century Europeans decided that American Indians were not completely human. The same was said at other times of blacks, Chinese, Hindus, and other groups. Dehumanization through difference: if they are not like us, they are not men. In the nineteenth century Hegel and Marx studied another variety based not on difference but on alienation. For Hegel alienation is as old as the human species: it began at the dawn of history with the subjugation of slave to master. Marx discovered yet another variety, that of the wage earner: the placing of a person in an abstract category that deprives him of his individuality. Slave or worker, the human person is reduced to a thing, a tool. The Nazis and Communists carried this psychic mutilation to its ultimate conclusion. The two totalitarianisms proposed to abolish the uniqueness and diversity of individuals: the Nazis, in the name of a biological absolute, race; the Communists, in the name of a historical absolute, class. Today, in the name of science, the goal is not the extermination of this or that group of individuals but the mass production of androids. Among the novels that predict the future, the one that most resembles our world today is not Orwell's *Nineteen Eighty-Four* but Huxley's *Brave New World.* Technological slavery is within sight. The human person survived two totalitarianisms: will it survive the domination of the world by technology?

My long digression has come to an end. Its conclusion is brief: the ills that afflict modern society are political and economic, but they are moral and spiritual as well, threatening the foundation of our civilization: the idea of the human person. That idea has been the source of political and intellectual freedoms; it has also been the creator of one of the great human inventions —love. The political and social reform of liberal capitalist democracies must be accompanied by a no less urgent reform of contemporary thought. Kant devoted himself to the critique of pure reason and practical reason; today we need another Kant to carry out the critique of scientific reason. This is a propitious moment, since in many of the sciences—as far as we laymen can judge—a noticeable movement of self-reflection and self-criticism is under way. A good example is modern cosmology. The dialogue between science, philosophy, and poetry could be the prelude to the reconstitution of the unity of culture. The prelude, as well, of the resurrection of the human person, who has been the cornerstone and wellspring of our civilization.

---

1. Alan Lightman and Roberta Brower, *Origins* (Cambridge, Mass., Harvard University Press, 1990).

2. I commented on Crick's book in a short essay written in 1982: "Extraterrestrial Intelligences and Demiurges, Bacteria and Dinosaurs." It was included in the collected volume *Sombras de obras* (1985). See *Excursiones/Incursiones,* vol. 2 of the Spanish edition of my *Obras Completas.*

3. T. S. Eliot, *Collected Poems 1909–1962* (New York: Harcourt Brace Jovanovich, 1963).

4. G. M. Edelman, *Bright Air, Bright Fire, On the Matter of the Mind* (New York: Basic Books, 1993).

5. Oliver Sacks, "Making up the Mind," *The New York Review of Books,* April 8, 1993.

6. Sacks, "Making up the Mind."

7. See my *Conjunctions and Disjunctions* (New York: Viking, 1974), also *The Other Voice* (New York: Harcourt Brace Jovanovich, 1991). Both translated by Helen Lane.

Recapitulation:
The Double Flame

EVERY DAY WE hear this phrase: Ours is the age of communication. A platitude which, like every other, involves an ambiguity. The modern news media are prodigious, but our use of those media, of the news and information transmitted by them, are not. The media often manipulate information, and, what is more, they inundate us with trivialities. But even without these defects, every communication, including the sort that is direct and without intermediaries, is equivocal. A dialogue, which is the highest form of communication we know, is always a confrontation of irreducibly different viewpoints. Its contradictory nature lies in the fact that it is an exchange of concrete, unique pieces of information for the person who voices them, and of abstract, general ones for the person who hears them. I say *green,* referring to a particular sensation, unique and inseparable from a specific instant, place, and psychological-physical state: the light falling on green ivy on this rather chilly spring afternoon. My partner in the dialogue hears a series of sounds and conjures up a vague idea of *green.* Are there possibilities of genuine communication? Yes, despite the fact that the fuzziness never entirely disappears. We are human beings, not angels. The senses connect us to the world and simultaneously shut us up inside ourselves: sensations are subjective and inexpressible. Thought and language are bridges, but, precisely because they are bridges, they do not erase the distance between ourselves and outer reality. With this reservation it can be said that poetry, fiesta, and love are forms of genuine communication, that is to say, of communion. Another difficulty: communion is inexpressible, and to a certain extent it excludes communication; it is not an exchange of news but a fusion. In the case of poetry, communion begins in a zone of silence, at the very moment the poem ends. A poem could be defined as a verbal organism that produces silence. In fiesta—I am thinking mainly of rites and religious ceremonies—the fusion takes place in the opposite direction: not a return to silence, the refuge of subjectivity, but a joining of the great collective whole—the *I* becomes a *we*. In love the contradiction between communication and communion is even more striking.

An erotic encounter begins with the sight of the desired body. Whether clothed or naked, the body is a presence: a form that for an instant is every form in the world. The moment we embrace that form, we cease to perceive it as a presence and grasp it as concrete, palpable matter, matter that fits within our arms and is nonetheless unlimited. But, embracing the presence, we no longer see that palpable matter. Dispersion of the desired body: all we see are a pair of eyes looking at us, a throat illuminated by the light of a lamp and soon disappearing into darkness again, the gleam of a thigh, the shadow descending from navel to genitals. Each of these fragments exists in and of itself yet refers to the totality of a body. A body which suddenly has become infinite. The body of my partner ceases to be a form and becomes an immense thing in which I both lose and recover myself. We lose ourselves as persons and recover ourselves as sensations. As sensation becomes more intense, the body we embrace becomes more immense. A sensation of infinity: we lose our body in that body. The carnal embrace is the apogee of the body and the loss of the body. It is also the experience of the loss of identity: a diffusion of form into a thousand sensations and visions, a fall into an ocean, an evaporation of essence. There is neither form nor presence: there is the wave that rocks us, the gallop across the plains of night. A circular experience: it begins with the abolition of the body of the couple, is transformed into an infinite substance that palpitates, expands, contracts, and enfolds us in primordial waters: an instant later the substance vanishes, the body becomes a body once again, and presence reappears. We can perceive the beloved only as a form that conceals an irreducible otherness or as a substance that cancels itself out and cancels us out.

The condemnation of carnal love as a sin against the spirit is not Christian in origin but Platonic. For Plato the form is the idea, the essence. The body is a presence in the true meaning of the word: the perceptible manifestation of essence. It is a likeness, the copy of a divine archetype: the eternal idea. Hence in the *Phaedrus* and the *Symposium* the highest love is the contemplation of a beautiful body: an ecstatic contemplation of a form that is essence. The carnal embrace involves a degen-

eration of form into substance and of idea into sensation. For the same reason Eros is invisible; he is not a
presence: he is the pulsing darkness that surrounds Psyche and drags her down in an endless fall. The lover
sees presence bathed in the light of the idea; he wants
to grasp it but falls into the darkness of a body that
breaks into fragments. Presence denies its form, returns
to its original substance—in order, in the end, to destroy itself. Destruction of presence, dissolution of form:
a sin against essence. Every sin entails a punishment:
once we have emerged from our ecstatic trance, we find
ourselves again in the presence of a body and soul that
are alien. Then the ritual question: What are you thinking about? And the reply: Nothing. Words that are
repeated in endless galleries of echoes.

It is not to be wondered that Plato condemned physical love. On the other hand he did not condemn reproduction. In the *Symposium* he calls the desire to
procreate divine: it is the yearning for immortality. The
offspring of the soul—ideas—are better, to be sure,
than flesh-and-blood offspring; but in the *Laws* he ex-
tols physical reproduction. The reason: it is a political
duty to engender citizens and women capable of en-
suring the continuity of life in the polis. Apart from
this ethical and political consideration, Plato clearly saw

the Panic side of love—its connection with the world of animal sexuality—and attempted to put an end to that. He was self-consistent; his vision of the world is of a piece with his philosophy of incorruptible ideas. But there is an irreconcilable contradiction in the Platonic conception of eroticism: without the body and the desire kindled in the lover there can be no ascent to the archetypes. To contemplate the eternal forms and participate in essence, it is necessary to pass by way of the body. There is no other path. In this respect Platonism is the opposite of the Christian vision: the Platonic eros seeks disincarnation, whereas Christian mysticism is, above all, a love of incarnation, following the example of Christ, who became flesh in order to save us. Despite this difference, both share the desire to break with this world and rise to the other: the Platonist by way of the ladder of contemplation, the Christian by way of love for a divinity which, although an ineffable mystery, assumed the form of a body.

United in their denial of this world, Platonism and Christianity differ on another fundamental point. In Platonic contemplation there is participation but no reciprocity: the eternal forms do not love humankind. The Christian God, on the other hand, suffers for humanity's sake because the Creator loves His creatures. By loving God, the theologians and mystics say, we return to Him, although in scant measure, the immense love He has for us. Human love, such as we know and live it in the West since the era of courtly love, arose from the convergence of Platonism and Christianity, and from their oppositions as well. Human love—that is to say, true love—denies neither the body nor the world. Nor does it aspire to any other world or see itself as a passage to a place beyond time and change. Love is love not *of* this world but *from* this world, bound to the earth by the body's gravitation, which is pleasure and death. Without a soul—or whatever one calls the *pneuma* that makes of every man and woman a person—there is no love, but neither is there love without a body. Through the body love is eroticism and thus communicates with the vastest and most deeply hidden forces of life. Both love and eroticism—the double flame—are fed by the original fire: sexuality. Love and eroticism always return to the primordial source, to Pan and his cry that makes the forest tremble.

The reverse of the Platonic eros is Tantrism in its two great branches: the Hindu and the Buddhist. For the disciple of Tantra the body does not manifest essence; it is a path of initiation. What lies beyond it is not essence, which for Plato is an object of contempla-

tion and participation: at the end of the erotic experience the devotee, if a Buddhist, arrives at emptiness, a
state in which being and nothingness are identical; if a
Hindu, a similar state is attained, but one in which the
important element is not nothingness but being—a being always identical to itself, beyond change. A twofold
paradox: for the Buddhist practitioner nothingness is
full; for the Hindu, being is empty. The central rite of
Tantrism is copulation. To possess a body, to go
through all the stages of the erotic embrace, not excluding any deviation or aberration, is to repeat as ritual
the cosmic process of creation, destruction, and re-
creation of worlds. It is also a way of breaking with
this process and stopping the wheel of time and successive reincarnations. The yogin avoids ejaculation,
with two objectives: denying the reproductive function
of sexuality, and transforming his semen into illuminated thought. An erotic alchemy: the fusion of ego and
world, thought and reality produces a blinding flash of
illumination, a burst of flame that literally consumes
subject and object. Nothing is left; the yogin has dis-
solved into the unconditional. The annihilation of
forms. In Tantrism there is a metaphysical violence absent in Platonism: breaking the cosmic cycle to enter
the unconditional. Ritual copulation is an immersion in

chaos, a return to the original source of life; but it is also an ascetic practice, a purification of the senses and the mind, a progressive stripping naked until annihilation is reached. The yogin keeps his distance from any amorous caress, and his physical enjoyment, ever more concentrated, is transformed into supreme indifference. A curious parallel with Sade, who saw in libertinage a path leading to ataraxia, the insensitivity of volcanic rock.

The differences between Tantrism and Platonism are instructive. The Platonic lover contemplates form, the body, without being tempted into an embrace; the yogin attains liberation through copulation. In the one case, contemplation of form is a journey that leads to the vision of essence and participation in it; in the other, ritual copulation requires that the darkness of eroticism be traversed and the destruction of forms realized. Despite its being a definitely carnal rite, Tantric eroticism is an experience of disincarnation. Platonism implies a repression and sublimation: the beloved form is untouchable and therefore removed from the realm of sadistic aggression. The yogin aspires to abolish desire and hence the contradictory nature of his attempt: it is an ascetic eroticism, a pleasure that the yogin denies himself. His experience is imbued with a sadism that is not physical but mental: forms must be destroyed. In Platonism, the beloved body is untouchable; in Tantrism, what is untouchable is the spirit of the yogin. Therefore he must tolerate, during the carnal embrace, all the caresses prescribed by the manuals of erotology, but while doing so he must retain his semen. If he succeeds in this, he achieves the indifference of the diamond: impenetrable, luminous, transparent.

Although the differences between Platonism and Tantrism are profound—they contain radically different visions of the world and humankind—there is a point at which they meet: the Other disappears. Both the body that the Platonic lover contemplates and the woman who embraces the yogin are objects, steps in an ascent toward the pure heaven of essences, or toward that region shown on no map, the unconditional. The end that both pursue lies beyond the Other. And this is essentially what separates them from love, as love has been described in these pages. It is worth repeating the point: love is not the search for the idea or the essence; neither is it a path toward a state transcending idea and nonidea, good and evil, being and nonbeing. Love seeks nothing beyond itself—no good, no reward. It does not pursue a final aim above it. It is indifferent to any sort of transcendence: it begins and ends in itself. It is an attraction exerted by a soul and a body, not by an idea. By a person. That person is unique and endowed with freedom; in order to possess that person, the lover must win over that person's will. Possession and surrender are reciprocal acts.

LIKE ALL THE great creations of humanity, love is twofold: it is the supreme happiness and the supreme misfortune. Abelard called the account of his life *The Story of My Calamities*. His greatest calamity was also his greatest happiness: to have met Eloise and been loved by her. Because of her he was a man: he knew love. And because of her he ceased to be a man: they castrated him. Abelard's story is a strange one, out of the ordinary; but in all love relations, without exception, such contrasts appear—though they are usually not as sharp. Lovers pass constantly from rapture to despair, from sadness to joy, from wrath to tenderness, from desperation to sensuality. Unlike the libertine, who simultaneously seeks the most intense pleasure and the greatest moral insensitivity, the lover is perpetually driven by contradictory emotions. Popular language, in all times and places, abounds in expressions that describe the vulnerability of a person in love: love is a wound, an injury. But as St. John of the Cross says, it is "a wound that is a gift," a "gentle cautery," a "delightful wound." Yes, love is a flower of blood. It is also a talisman: the vulnerability of lovers protects them. Their shield is their lack of defense; their armor is their nakedness. A cruel paradox: the extreme sensitivity of lovers is the reverse side of their indifference, no less extreme, toward everything that is not their love. The great danger that trips up lovers, the deadly trap into which many fall, is self-absorption. The punishment is not long in coming: they see nothing and no one except themselves, until they turn to stone . . . or grow bored. Self-absorption is a well. In order to emerge into the open air, we must look beyond ourselves: that is where the world is, and it awaits us.

Love does not preserve us from the risks and misfortunes of existence. No love, not even those that are the most peaceful and happy, escapes the disasters and calamities of time. Love, any love, is made up of time, and no love can avoid the great catastrophe: the beloved is subject to the assaults of age, infirmity, and death. As a remedy against time and the seduction of love, Buddhists conceived a meditation practice that consisted of imagining the body of a woman as a sack of filth. Christian monks practiced similar exercises in denigration of life. This remedy was ineffective and brought on the vengeance of the body and exasperated imagination: the temptations, at once terrifying and lascivious, of the anchorites. Their visions, though but shadows made of air, phantoms that the light dispels, are not chimeras: they are realities which live in the psychic subsoil and which abstinence nourishes and strengthens. Transformed into monsters by imagination, they are unleashed by desire. Each of the creatures that people the hell of St. Anthony is an emblem of a repressed passion. The negation of life turns into violence. Abstinence does not free us of time; it transforms it into psychic aggression, against others and against ourselves.

There is no remedy for time. Or, at least, we do not know what it is. But we must trust in the flow of time, we must live. The body ages because it is time, as does everything that exists on this earth. I am well aware that we have succeeded in prolonging life and youth. For Balzac the critical age for a woman began at thirty; today it begins at fifty. Many scientists believe that in the not too distant future it will be possible to avoid the ailments of old age. This optimistic prediction stands in contrast to what we know and see every day; poverty is increasing on more than half the planet, there are famines, and in the former Soviet Union, in the final years of the Communist regime, the rate of infant mortality rose. (One of the causes of the collapse of the Soviet empire.) But even if the optimists are right, we will continue to be subject to time. We are time and cannot escape its dominion. We can transfigure it but not deny it or destroy it. This is what the great artists, poets, philosophers, scientists, and certain men of action have done. Love, too, is an answer: because it is time and made of time, love is at once consciousness of death and an attempt to make of the instant an eternity. All loves are ill-starred, because all are made of time, all are the fragile bond between two temporal creatures who know they are going to die. In all loves, even the most tragic, there is an instant of happiness that it is no exaggeration to call superhuman: it is a victory over time, a glimpse of the other side, of the there that is a here, where nothing changes and everything that is, truly is.

Youth is the time of love. But there are old young people incapable of love—not because of sexual impotence but from an aridity of soul. There are also young old people who fall in love—some are ridiculous, some pathetic, and some sublime. But can we love a body that has grown old or been disfigured by disease? It is very difficult but not entirely impossible. We should remember that eroticism is singular and finds no anomaly contemptible. Aren't there beautiful monsters? It is also true that we can go on loving a person despite the erosion of habit and daily life, or the ravages of old age and infirmity. In such cases physical attraction ceases and love is transformed. In general it turns not into pity but compassion, in the sense of sharing another's suffering. When he was already an old man, Unamuno said: "I do not feel anything when I brush against the legs of my wife, but mine ache if hers do." The word *passion* also means suffering, and in this way too it designates the sentiment of love. Love is suffering and heartache, because it is a lack and the desire to possess what we lack; in turn, it is happiness, because it is possession, even though the possession lasts but a moment. The *Diccionario de Autoridades* records another word no longer in use today but one employed by Petrarch: *compathía,* which might be translated as shared suffering. It is a forceful expression of that sentiment of love transfigured by the old age or infirmity of the beloved.

According to tradition, love is an indefinable amalgam of soul and body; between them, like a fan, a series of sentiments and emotions unfold, ranging from the most direct sexuality to veneration, from tenderness to eroticism. Many of those sentiments are negative; love includes rivalry, spite, fear, jealousy, and, lastly, hatred.

As Catullus wrote long ago: "Hatred is indistinguishable from love." These feelings of affection and resentment, these sympathies and antipathies are commingled in all amorous relationships and make a unique liquor, which is different in every case and changes color, aroma, and flavor as time, circumstances, and moods change. It is a philter more powerful than the one imbibed by Tristan and Isolde. It brings life and death—everything depends on the lovers. It may become passion, boredom, affection, obsession. In old age it may turn into *compathía*. How to define this feeling? It is not an affect of the head or of the genitals but of the heart. It is the last fruit of love, when habit, ennui, and that insidious temptation that makes us hate everything we once loved have been overcome.

Love is intensity and therefore a distension of time: it stretches minutes to centuries. Linear time becomes discontinuous and immeasurable. But after each of these immeasurable instants we return to time and its regular intervals: we cannot escape succession. Love begins with a look: we gaze at the person to whom we are attracted, and he or she gazes back. What is it we see? Everything and nothing. After a moment we avert our eyes. Otherwise we would be turned to stone. In "The Extasie," one of his most complex poems, Donne describes this situation. Enraptured, the lovers look at each other interminably:

> Wee, like sepulchrall statues lay;
> All day, the same our postures were,
> And we said nothing, all the day . . .

If this immobile beatitude were prolonged, we would perish. We must return to our bodies; life reclaims us.

> Love's mysteries in soules doe grow,
> But yet the body is his booke.

We must look, together, at the world that surrounds us. We must go farther, until we encounter the unknown.

If love is time, it cannot be eternal. It is doomed to die or be transformed into another feeling. The story of Philemon and Baucis recounted by Ovid in Book VIII of his *Metamorphoses* is a charming example. Jupiter and Mercury are traveling through Phrygia, but they find no hospitality in any of the houses where they seek shelter, until they reach the humble dwelling of an old man, the poor and pious Philemon, and his wife Baucis. The couple generously welcomes them, offers them a crude bed of seaweed and a frugal meal washed down with new wine drunk from wooden cups. Gradually the two old people realize the divine nature of their guests and prostrate themselves before them. The gods reveal their identity and order the couple to come with them to the top of a nearby hill. Then, with a sign, they cause water to cover the earth of the impious Phrygians and turn their houses and fields to ruins. From the hilltop Baucis and Philemon look with fear and pity on the destruction of their neighbors; then, with amazement, they see how their hut has been transformed into a marble temple with a gold roof. Jupiter asks them to tell him their fondest wish. Philemon exchanges a few words with Baucis, then asks that the gods allow them to be the guardians and priests of this temple as long as the two of them live. He adds: Because we have lived together since we were young, we wish to die together at the same moment. "May I not see the funeral pyre of Baucis nor she bury me." And so it was: they were caretakers of the temple for many years until, worn out by time, each saw the other become covered with leaves. They said at the same moment, "Farewell, my spouse," and bark sealed their mouths. Philemon and Baucis had turned into trees: an oak and a linden. Time did not vanquish them; they yielded to its flow and hence transformed it and transformed themselves.

Philemon and Baucis did not ask for immortality, did not wish to go beyond the human condition: they accepted it, they surrendered to time. The miraculous metamorphosis with which the gods—time—rewarded them was a return: they returned to nature, to share with it, in it, the successive transformations of everything that lives. Thus their story offers us, at this end of a century, another lesson. In antiquity the belief in metamorphosis was founded on the continuous communication between three worlds: the supernatural, the human, and the natural. Rivers, trees, hills, forests, seas, everything was animate, everything communicated with everything else, and everything was transformed by this communication. Christianity desacralized nature and drew an impassable line dividing the natural and the human. The nymphs fled, the naiads, satyrs, and Tritons were turned into angels or demons. The modern age accentuated the divorce: at one extreme, nature, and at the other, culture. Today, as modernity comes to an end, we are rediscovering that we are part of nature. The earth is a system of relationships or, as the Stoics put it, a "conspiration of elements" all moved by universal sympathy. We are parts, living pieces of that system. The idea of humanity's kinship with the universe appears at the very origin of the idea of love. It is a belief that begins with the first poets, suffuses Romantic poetry, and has been handed down to us. The kinship between a mountain and a woman or between a tree and a man are focal points of the feeling of love. Today love can be, as it was in the past, a way of reconciliation with nature. We cannot change ourselves into springs or oak trees, birds or bulls, but we can *recognize ourselves* in them.

No less sad than seeing the person we love grow old and die is the discovery that our lover is betraying us or has stopped loving us. Subject to time, change, and death, love can also fall victim to boredom. Living together day after day, if lovers lack imagination, can bring the most intense love to an end. We have little power against the misfortunes that time has in store for every man and woman. Life is a continual risk; to live is to expose oneself. The hermit's abstinence turns into a solitary delirium, the lovers' flight into a cruel death. Other passions can seduce us and enthrall us: some of them lofty, such as the love of God, of knowledge, or of a cause; others base, such as the love of money or power. In none of these passions does the risk inherent in life disappear. The mystic may discover that he has been pursuing an illusion; knowledge does not protect the wise man from the disappointment that all learning yields; power does not save the politician from betrayal by a friend. Glory is a frequently miscalculated goal, and oblivion can get the better of any reputation. The misfortunes of love are simply the adversities of life.

Yet despite all the ills and misfortunes it brings, we always endeavor to love and be loved. Love is the closest thing on this earth to the beatitude of the blessed. The images of the golden age and earthly paradise are mixed with those of love that is returned: the couple in the bosom of a reconciled nature. For more than two millennia, in the West as in the East, imagination has created ideal pairs of lovers that are the crystallization of our desires, dreams, fears, and obsessions. The couples are almost always young: Daphnis and Chloe, Calixto and Melibea, Bao-yu and Dai-yu. A notable exception is Philemon and Baucis. Symbols of love, these couples enjoy a superhuman happiness but also come to a tragic end. Antiquity saw in love a fit of delirium, and even Ovid, the great singer of frivolous love affairs, devoted an entire book, *The Heroides,* to the misfortunes of love: separation, absence, betrayal. The book consists of twenty-one epistles written by famous women to the lovers and husbands, all legendary heroes, who abandoned them. But for antiquity the archetype was the young and blissful pair: Daphnis and Chloe, Eros and Psyche. The Middle Ages, however, tended toward the tragic model. The poem of Tristan begins as follows: "Sirs, would it please you to hear a fine story of love and death? It is the story of Tristan and Isolde the queen. Listen to how, amid great joys and sorrows, they loved each other and died that very day, he for her and she for him. . . ." From the Renaissance on, the model has also been tragic: Calixto and Melibea, but first and foremost *Romeo and Juliet,* the saddest of all these stories, for the two innocents die as victims not of fate but of chance. With Shakespeare, accident dethrones the Destiny of the ancients and the Providence of Christianity.

There is a couple—Adam and Eve—that includes all couples, from the elderly Philemon and Baucis to the adolescent Romeo and Juliet; their image and story are those of the human condition in all times and places. They are the first couple. Although a Judeo-Christian myth, Adam and Eve have equivalents or counterparts in other religions. They live in paradise, a place that is not beyond time but at its beginning. Paradise is what has been *before*; history is the deterioration of primordial time, the fall of the eternal present into succession.

Before history, in paradise, nature was innocent and every creature lived in harmony with every other, in harmony with itself and with the whole. Sin casts Adam and Eve into successive time: into change, accident, work, and death. Nature, having been corrupted, becomes divided, and the enmity between creatures begins, the universal slaughter: all against all. Adam and Eve wander through this cruel and hostile world, people it with their deeds and dreams, wet it with their tears and the sweat of their brow. They know the glory of making and procreating, of the work that exhausts the body, of the years that cloud the sight and spirit, of the horror of the son who dies and the son who is killed; they eat the bread of sorrow and drink the water of happiness. Time dwells within them, and time abandons them. Every pair of lovers relives their story, every couple suffers the nostalgia for paradise, every couple is aware of death and experiences a continual bodily struggle against time, which has no body. . . . To reinvent love is to reinvent the original couple, the two creatures exiled from Eden, the two creators of this world and of history.

Love does not defeat death; it is a wager against time and its accidents. Through love we catch a glimpse, in this life, of the other life. Not of eternal life, but, as I have tried to say in several poems, of pure vitality. Speaking of the religious experience, Freud refers to an "oceanic feeling," that sensation of being enveloped in and rocked by all of existence. It is the Panic dimension of the ancients, the sacred *furor,* enthusiasm: the recovery of wholeness and the discovery of the self as a wholeness within the Great Whole. When we were born, we were torn from wholeness; in love we have all felt ourselves returning to the original wholeness. That is why poetic images transform the beloved into nature—a mountain, water, a cloud, a star, a wood, the sea, a wave—and why in turn nature speaks as though it were a lover. Reconciliation with the totality of the world. With past, present, and future as well. Love is not eternity; nor is it the time of calendars and watches, successive time. The time of love is neither great nor small; it is the perception of all times, of all lives, in a single instant. It does not free us from death but makes us see it face to face. That instant is the reverse and complement of the "oceanic feeling." It is not the return to the waters of origin but the attainment of a state that reconciles us to our having been driven out of paradise. We are the theater of the embrace of opposites and of their dissolution, resolved in a single note that is not affirmation or negation but acceptance. What does the couple see in the space of an instant, a blink of the eye? The equation of appearance and disappearance, the truth of the body and the nonbody, the vision of the presence that dissolves into splendor: pure vitality, a heartbeat of time.